CU00829240

The Good and the Good Book

"*The Good and the Good Book: Revelation as a Guide to Life* is a constructive, reflective, and highly personal meditation on belief, religion, and the good life by a scholar and believer deeply engaged in modern philosophical and theological thought. Written almost like a spiritual memoir, Sam Fleischacker takes his reader through a series of theological challenges that face anyone invested in 'revealed religion' who is equally concerned about tolerance and pluralism, and presents a case where revealed religion can survive its modern critique. *The Good and the Good Book* is a work of very accessible philosophical theology that should be of interest to scholars of religion, constructive theologians, and anyone struggling with living inside a religious tradition in these troubling times."

Shaul Magid, Indiana University

"Sam Fleischacker has given us a conceptual tour de force that illuminates the path for those seeking to have an ethical faith that is grounded in revelation. Lesser thinkers choose only one side of the tension or create false harmonies. In contrast, Fleischacker carefully untangles the knotty issues then he boldly and cogently shows a path of combining Divine teachings based on revelation with liberal virtues and modern science. The book deserves a broad reception and engagement with its timely ideas."

Alan Brill, Seton Hall University

The Good and the Good Book

Revelation as a Guide to Life

Samuel Fleischacker

OXFORD
UNIVERSITY PRESS

Great Clarendon Street, Oxford, OX2 6DP,
United Kingdom

Oxford University Press is a department of the University of Oxford.
It furthers the University's objective of excellence in research, scholarship,
and education by publishing worldwide. Oxford is a registered trade mark of
Oxford University Press in the UK and in certain other countries

First Edition published in 2015

Impression: 1

Published in the United States of America by Oxford University Press
198 Madison Avenue, New York, NY 10016, United States of America

British Library Cataloguing in Publication Data

Data available

Library of Congress Control Number: 2014954756

ISBN 978-0-19-873307-2

Printed and bound by
CPI Group (UK) Ltd, Croydon, CR0 4YY

Acknowledgments

I might not have written this book at all had I not been urged by Bronwyn Rae, Amy Reichert, and Alan Brill to produce a shorter, more accessible version of my earlier book on revelation, *Divine Teaching and the Way of the World*. In addition, Amy, Bronwyn, and Alan, along with Bob Fischer and Michael Balinsky, read large parts of the manuscript and made excellent suggestions for improving it. My heartfelt thanks to all of them for that. I'd also like to thank the students in Jay Bruce's class on the philosophy of religion at John Brown University, who read two chapters of the manuscript and responded with terrifically astute questions—and of course to thank Jay himself, for inviting me to his class.

I am grateful to the Center for Advanced Study in the Behavioral Sciences for providing a serene environment in which to do the final revisions of this book, and to Peter Momtchiloff—a wonderfully supportive and encouraging editor.

A breakfast with Jay Shefsky, in which he asked me to explain my commitment to traditional Judaism, led me to realize that I didn't have good answers to his questions. Both *Divine Teaching* and this book grew out of an effort to improve on what I said to Jay. I remain grateful to this day for his questions.

A talk by Daniel Statman, on the independence of morality from religion, helped spark my thoughts on what, if not morality, religion is good for. Conversations with Gershom Gorenberg, Mark Rosen, and Kelley Jolley, have also helped me in many ways.

In addition to reading and helping me edit this manuscript, my wife Amy Reichert has been throughout a steadfast source of love and support, as she always is. No words can express my gratitude to her.

S.F.

Evanston, Illinois

Table of Contents

Introduction

My wife and I took a long honeymoon in 1990, which was supposed to end with a four-month stay in Israel. We arrived in Israel on 3 August, the day after Saddam Hussein invaded Kuwait. Shortly thereafter, Saddam threatened to send gas-tipped missiles into Israel if the US took military action against him. My in-laws, extremely safety-conscious in the best of times, immediately began to pressure us to leave. I was appalled at that idea. Long a supporter of Israel's *Peace Now* movement, I had been dogged for years by the question, "How can you urge Israelis to take risks for peace when you yourself live safely in America, and don't have to share those risks?" So I welcomed the opportunity to share a danger Israel faced, and felt I would convict myself of cowardice if I left. Besides, we had found a lovely apartment in Jerusalem and I wanted to introduce my wife to the joys of that city, and of living in a majority-Jewish environment. I therefore refused to leave. My wife was torn between my views, which she respected but did not entirely share, and the call of her parents.

Thus things stood for a week or two, while the pressure from my in-laws grew steadily. I felt firm in my decision to stay; I was even ready to end my new marriage, if necessary, for the sake of what I took to be a crucial test of my courage and commitments. Then one morning, after a particularly difficult run of phone calls from America, I came across the following line, in the traditional Torah reading for the week: "When a man has taken a new wife, he shall not go out to war . . . but he shall be free at home one year, and shall cheer his wife whom he has taken." (Deuteronomy 24:5) The relevance of this line to my own situation seemed unmistakable. I took God to be speaking directly to me—and, rather to my surprise, taking the side of my relatively secular in-laws. Whatever the circumstances in which the passage was originally written, right then and right there it served as God's word to me, telling me to get off my high horse about my supposed courage and commitments, and to attend to my wife and our marriage. So we left Israel. I felt very bitter about this decision. But who am I to argue with God? And I believe that God speaks to me through the Torah.

A story like this raises a host of issues. Here are just a few:

(1) Would I or any other religious person really want to say that any verse we happen to stumble over, in our sacred texts, should guide our actions? What if I had come across one of the verses in the Torah calling for idolaters to be killed? Would I have rushed out to fulfill that command? The answer, of course, is "Certainly not," but that simply shows that even devout believers bring certain moral principles or attitudes to their sacred text, and figure out how to follow it in that light. In this case, it matters that I could see my wife's and wife's family's concerns as morally respectable, for all that I disagreed with them, even before I encountered the verse that led me to my decision. So I did not rely on the Torah alone in making my decision: I needed a moral prism, independent of the Torah, to determine what it was saying.

(2) I needed to do other interpretive work as well to see the verse I came across as addressing my situation. I was *not* after all heading off to war, merely staying in a country that might come under military threat. Nor is the command exempting new husbands from military duty understood by the Jewish tradition to apply to wars of self-defense. So although it is understandable, I think, why I took Deuteronomy 24:5 to be addressing me, I did *choose to take* the verse that way. There are choices about how to interpret it, and it could be read very differently.

(3) The two questions I have thus far raised bring out the degree to which sacred or revealed texts shape a believer's life only via a particular way of receiving that text (the topic of Chapter 6 of this book) and for many believers, in many religions, that way does not much consist in the sort of direct, personal response I have described. Traditional Judaism indeed discourages such responses. The story I have told is more characteristic of how certain Protestants respond to the Bible—Christians who, for reasons rooted in a theology very different from that of most Jews, think

we should as much as possible do without mediation between Holy Scripture and its readers. Jews, by contrast, like Catholics and Muslims, emphasize the importance of a community and tradition in the reception of sacred texts, and urge one another to hear God's word through that sort of mediation. Even in these traditions, there may remain a role for God to speak to us individually through our texts, but we are taught to be wary of thinking we have had such a communication, and to fit anything we think we have learned that way into accepted communal and traditional practices.

(4) All these problems pale before the basic question of why any sensible person in the modern day would dream of supposing that the Torah, or any other traditional teaching or text, really comes from God. Do I really believe that the Torah was written by Moses at God's dictation, and has come down to us in an unbroken chain ever since? Do I believe that God spoke on Sinai in thunder and fire? Even if there is a God—and that's a big "if"— the idea that that God wrote the Torah seems patently absurd, in the light of what we now know about its authorship, let alone about the physics and biology that it ignores or defies.

I do not plan to defend the Torah's scientific or historical accuracy; I will indeed argue that one can suppose the Torah to be highly *in*accurate, scientifically and historically, yet still regard it as God's word. Nor do I think that Jews need to show the Torah to be superior to all other putatively revealed texts in order to take it as God's word. They can instead regard it, as I did in the story above, as God's way of speaking *to them*, while leaving open the possibility that God has other ways of speaking to other people. That is to say: other people can just as reasonably regard *their* sacred texts as scientifically and historically inaccurate, but nevertheless God's word to them (or in some other way their source of supreme ethical wisdom).

All these claims no doubt seem puzzling and unpersuasive, when asserted thus briefly. The purpose of this book is to expand and defend them, although I do not provide anything close to a knockdown argument for them. Religious commitment does not on my view follow primarily from rational argument: it depends on a non-rational faith or trust, and one of my main purposes is indeed to elucidate why a reasonable person might adopt a non-rational faith or trust. I want, centrally, to explain why it might be reasonable to place such a non-rational faith or trust in the teaching of a *text*, passed down by a community as sacred like the "good book" of my title, rather than in the glimpses of the divine one might think to attain by way of personal experience or intuition. Texts form the focus of revealed religions, and it is the reverent attitude towards them that especially irritates modern liberal and scientifically-minded people. Two centuries ago, Kant already complained about people who say "It is written" when asked to explain what they do, and that complaint continues to be made, widely, by critics of traditional religions.

The emphasis on a text is particularly important to traditional *Judaism*, of course, and there are other religious believers who would say that revelation takes a different form for them. Many Christians might say that revelation for them takes place primarily in the life of Jesus, or in their relationship to him, not in the New Testament, while immediate experience at a shrine or in a home ritual may be a prime source of revelation for a Hindu. Still, even here a central text tends to inform how the significance of Jesus, or of the ritual experience, is understood. Thus a Christian will normally say that the life of Jesus, or her relationship to Jesus, reveals him as *God*, not just as a prophet or a sage; a Christian will, that is, normally understand Jesus, and her relationship with Jesus, by way of the New Testament. Similarly, a Hindu will normally understand any mystical insight she experiences by way of the Vedas and Upanishads. So even though other traditions may not emphasize a text as explicitly as Jews do, a sacred text or set of texts does play a defining role in practically all traditional religions.

To work, now. The first problem we need to overcome, in rendering reverence for a religious text comprehensible, is why a truthful God (or other source of supreme wisdom) might communicate with us through a text that seems filled with blatant falsehoods. We will find it useful for this purpose to expand the notion of "truth" with which we usually work; that is the subject of Chapter 1.

One might imagine that the expansion in question will take the form of saying that sacred texts deal with ethical rather than scientific truth. That's not quite right, however, since we come to most moral principles—the core of what we mean by "ethics"—independently of religious revelation. What is revealed to us is not exactly morality but *the overall good* of our lives. Sorting out morality from our overall good is the subject of Chapters 2 and 3.

I turn in Chapter 4 to why revelation might give us access to our overall good. The remaining chapters concern how my account of revelation makes sense of belief in God, an afterlife, and the other metaphysical mysteries that normally go with revealed religion (Chapter 5); what role it gives to the interpretation of revealed texts, to ritual practice, and to religious community (Chapter 6); and how it allows for believers in one religion to respect other sorts of believers, and secular people (Chapter 7). With all these pieces in hand, it will I hope be possible to see how commitment to a revealed religion can go along with a full acceptance of modern science and liberal morality.

Whether any particular revealed religion is worthy of such commitment is a further question which I do not try to address. I think that rational argument can do little to bring about religious commitment. Rational argument can lay out the framework within which a non-rational religious commitment makes sense, but revelation itself, if there is such a thing, must take us the rest of the way. Those of us who are committed to a revealed religion believe that something has been disclosed to us that rational argument alone cannot provide. We turn to rational argument just to help us figure out how this disclosure can be brought together with the aspects of our lives that must remain rational. The framework I sketch in this book is meant as a contribution to that endeavor.

1
Truth

Revealed religion stands in contrast, primarily, with rational or personal religion. Revealed religions don't simply argue for their central beliefs, as a purely rational religion would, nor do they urge believers to find spiritual meaning by way of meditation, mystical insight, or other forms of personal experience. Rather, they take their view of what the universe is fundamentally like, and what human beings ought to do in it, from something that they claim was taught by God, or by an extraordinary human being (Confucius, the Buddha, Lao-tzu) after a moment of extraordinary insight. This teaching is enshrined in a text or set of sayings that gets passed down, along with interpretations of it and a ritual practice said to derive from it, from generation to generation. "Passing down" in Latin is *traditio* and a religion that passes down its teachings and practices in this way may also be called a "traditional religion."

A revealed religion is, then, a religion centered around a text and a tradition. Almost everything we ordinarily call "religion"—Judaism, Islam, Hinduism—is a revealed or traditional religion; this is also what people mean when they talk of "organized religion." Indeed, even when groups break off from a traditional religion, rejecting its texts or practices as stifling to true spirituality, they tend to claim a new revelation of their own. This is the story of early Christianity; in more recent years the Christian Scientists have put up *Science and Health With a Key to the Scriptures* alongside the Bible and Mormons have added *The Book of Mormon*. Even the Bahais, who are committed to a search for truth free of tradition, have a series of texts that they regard as a new revelation. Aside from the practices of a few animist tribes that are too amorphous to be identified with a particular teaching, what the phrases "revealed religion" and "traditional religion" clearly exclude is just rational religion, to the extent that that exists, and personal religions of the sort associated with New Age spirituality. But over the past two centuries liberal or progressive branches of Judaism and Christianity have also tended to play down the importance of revelation and tradition, in favor of reason and personal experience. The idea that God's nature or will, or any other spiritually important fact, might be best disclosed in a text composed centuries ago makes people trained in modern science uneasy; reverence for an ancient text is also thought to entrench sexist, racist, and other prejudices.

These concerns are eminently reasonable. The idea that we should show reverence for an ancient text, and the teachings and practices passed down in its name, raises serious concerns for us moderns from both a scientific and a moral point of view. Nevertheless, my point in this book is to defend that idea. Indeed, I will offer reasons in defense of all the features of revealed religion that most offend secular people, and embarrass progressive believers: a sacred text, prescribed rituals, and the communal organizations that preserve these things. All these features flow from the idea of revelation, as I understand it—from the deference to sacred texts that defines traditional Christianity, Islam, Hinduism, and the like. And the scientific and moral concerns raised by the idea of revelation are answerable, although they require us to re-think what revelation is, to some degree. My main concern throughout this book is to lay out and defend this revised conception of revelation, not to argue against the non-revelatory sorts of religion taught by progressive churches and synagogues. I will not even argue, much, against a complete rejection of religion. I want to show simply that, if one is to be religious, one has good reason to revere a traditional religious text, and the teaching and practices associated with it.

One more introductory note. As I've indicated, I consider the notion of a revealed religion a broad one, which can include non-theistic traditions like Buddhism and Taoism as well as the so-called "Abrahamic" religions familiar to us in the West. But some followers of Eastern religions, especially Buddhism, do not see the texts they care about as revealed in any obvious sense. I don't want to dispute these issues here, and my focus is in fact primarily on theistic religions; I simply hope and believe that much of what I say will be transferable, with but minor changes, to religions like Buddhism and Taoism. Still, so as not to speak presumptuously about traditions I don't know well, for the most part I will talk of "God" in this book, and of people who speak for God rather than of sages, like the Buddha, whose teachings are not theistic. Indeed, I will draw many of my examples from the Jewish tradition, since I know it best.

To begin in earnest, now, what do believers mean by calling their sacred texts "true"? Given the obvious scientific errors and historical inaccuracies that fill practically every religious book, how can anyone regard them as true? Traditional Jews, Christians, and Muslims take their Bibles and Quran to be not just true but the *paradigm* of truth, the source of the highest wisdom human beings can attain. But surely we have every reason, today, to reject these claims. The Torah and the Gospels report all sorts of events that modern science considers impossible, and scientifically-minded historians have shown them to be riddled with historical inaccuracies. What on earth can a person mean, then, by calling them "true"? Of course, some believers mean that modern science is wrong, to the extent that it contradicts their sacred scripture, and that everything in the text is literally correct. But other believers are, I think, using the word "true" in a rather different way from the way it gets used in science: they are indeed challenging the monopoly that our society tends to grant science over that word.

Let us start our investigation with these issues. Consider first the people who suggest that modern science is wrong, insofar as it conflicts with the Bible. There are more and less sophisticated versions of this claim. Those who espouse the less sophisticated version may insist that fossil evidence is unreliable, or that the fossil evidence we have, properly read, is compatible with a 6000-year-old earth. Not unrelated, I think, are those who say they have scientific evidence of a special sort showing that the Bible is true: personal experiences of miraculous cures, say, or remarkable predictions of the sort that have been drawn from the so-called "Bible Code" (a numerological reading of the Bible that supposedly shows how the assassination of Yitzhak Rabin, for instance, was foreseen by Biblical verses). Some of these claims are flatly incorrect: fossil evidence is not compatible with a 6000-year-old earth, for instance. Others demonstrate a misunderstanding of the nature of science. Claims to the effect that evolution by natural selection is "just a theory," for instance, misunderstand what "theory" means in science (all science consists of theories: direct observations are themselves informed by theory, and have no scientific significance until they are combined, sifted, and explained by theories). The sorts of evidence that fans of the Bible Code produce—which depend pervasively on implausible readings, and lack any experimental control (for example an attempt to apply the same methods to texts other than the Bible)—demonstrate similar failures to understand how scientific evidence works. In any case, these claims are all overwhelmingly rejected by practicing scientists. Science is a social project, in which empirical evidence is gathered, tested, and analyzed by enormous numbers of trained people. So the fact that practically no respected expert in any relevant scientific field—no physicist, no biologist, no geologist—accepts today that the world was created 6000 years ago, or in six days, or with all species just as they are now, tells strongly against these claims. To stand against the overwhelming consensus of scientists on a matter of empirical fact is already to fail to appreciate scientific procedure; we have good reason to think that an overwhelming consensus of scientists, on a matter within their expertise, is likely to be correct.

All of which helps to explain why people trained in science tend quickly to dismiss those who enlist science in support of a Biblical faith. Perhaps too quickly. Scientific theories have after all come and gone many times in the course of human history, and supposed experts have often been massively wrong, even when they have agreed among themselves. Astrology, the four humors theory of medicine, and the idea that a flat earth lies at the center of the universe were all upheld with just the sort of overwhelming expert support that today is accorded to the Big Bang and evolution by natural selection. Yet they were nonetheless incorrect, and dissidents like Galileo were right to stand up against them. Why could the same not be true of today's consensus on evolution? How can anyone be confident that the religious dissidents who uphold a creationist theory, far from being crazy, are not the real Galileos of our time?

But the comparison is specious. It is true that many wildly incorrect theories, from geocentrism to the notion that stars are bodiless intelligences, dominated the world before the rise of modern science in the seventeenth century. Their dominance was however due largely to the fact that investigation of the world in pre-modern times was conducted under the threat of punishment for those who dissented from a religious party line. The method of investigation was also never carried out by way of the controlled experiments, the massive collection of data (aided by new technology like the microscope and telescope), and the powerful mathematical tools introduced by the likes of Descartes, Galileo, Huygens, Newton, and Lavoisier. Modern science is a radically novel way of investigating the universe, which has had an astounding, unprecedented predictive and technological payoff, and has become a self-correcting enterprise that overcomes its own failures quickly and easily. Certainly, it is subject to human error and prejudice, but it is so open, so competitive, and run by such large numbers of people, that it is extremely unlikely to maintain for long the kinds of dogmas that sustained astrology and geocentrism. On the contrary, it is those who insist on a 6000-year-old earth and the like who resemble the dogmatists of yore—who resemble the establishment that opposed Galileo.

I said there was a more sophisticated version of the "science may be wrong" view. This version accepts modern science, but denies that it has undermined the central claims of one or more religions. Arguments along these lines are found mostly among professional philosophers rather than in the general public, especially among a group of philosophers whom I will call "the new religious rationalists"; they include Alvin Plantinga, William Alston, Nicholas Wolterstorff, and Richard Swinburne. The new religious rationalists grant the basic claims of modern cosmology and biology (that the universe began with the Big Bang, almost fourteen billion years ago, and that life has developed by way of Darwinian evolution), and focus instead on the metaphysics *of* science. They have revived some medieval proofs of God, suggested that science itself may be unintelligible unless there is a God, and argued that scientific laws cannot show the impossibility of miracles. With these metaphysical results in hand, they also argue that modern scientific critics of the Bible—the so-called "higher critics," who assess the Bible using historical tools that draw on modern science—start from the dogmatic assumption that there could not possibly be miracles. Sometimes they add considerations meant to show that aspects of the Bible are likely to be true.

Some of these points are I think correct and important. It is true, I believe, that science cannot disprove the existence of God, or of miracles. It is also true that much scientific criticism of the Bible is governed by assumptions that prevent the critics from being able to see it as a record of real religious experience, and that the critics rarely make any attempt to justify these assumptions. These negative points—about what science cannot do—are moreover important to anyone who wants to entertain the possibility that the Bible, or any other Scripture, reveals God's nature or will.

But I don't go along with the positive program of the new religious rationalists. Like most philosophers, I don't find the proofs of God they have revived convincing, and am even less persuaded by the considerations they adduce for the likelihood that God would perform certain miracles. And even if they are right about the biases of modern Bible critics, the evidence for the historical inaccuracy of the Bible is so overwhelming that it is foolhardy to rest anything on its factual claims.

Let me therefore re-cast the good points of the new religious rationalists in terms somewhat different from their own. My view follows the teachings of Immanuel Kant, who argued that science can neither disprove nor prove the central principles of religion, and went on from there to an argument that religion, if true, must be so for reasons independent of science.

Whatever Richard Dawkins may say, science cannot rule out the existence of God. God, if He/She exists at all, must either pervade the entire empirical universe or lie beyond it; God cannot be something we might observe at some places and times but not at others, or Whose presence we could detect by a controlled experiment. To test the existence of God is to presume that there are things or realms independent of God, which can be compared to the things or realms that God has created; this is theological nonsense, at least for monotheists. So God is not the sort of being whose existence science can possibly determine—not the sort of being, indeed, that can *have* the sort of existence that objects of science have. Science studies things and forces *within* the natural world, limited aspects of that world that can be contrasted with other aspects. It can't get a grip on a being or force that is supposed to be equally present in all of nature, or that structures or runs the whole natural world without being part of any of it. So science can neither prove nor disprove the existence of God. Nor can it prove or disprove the existence of miracles, which are surely possible if there is a God (how could a being that governs all nature *not* be able to suspend the laws of nature?), and impossible if there is no God.

All this is true, at least, of *modern* science. Modern science is but one of many ways in which human beings have tried to explain the natural world, and some pre-modern theories of nature seemed to entail that there be a God. Aristotelian and neo-Platonic science, for instance, which dominated medieval worldviews in the West, required the postulate of a necessary and all-Good Being, from whom all other existence flows. Modern science requires no such thing.

That said, one science-oriented argument for belief in God given by the new religious rationalists strikes me as plausible. In several of his books, Alvin Plantinga has pointed out that there are good evolutionary arguments against the view that natural science can tell us everything about our world. Evolutionary accounts of the development of our mind suggest that we will be inclined to believe whatever is conducive to our survival. But adaptive beliefs of this sort need not line up with the truth. Much of the time it will be useful to our species, for instance, for us to believe that we will get through dangerous journeys or military exploits even if that is not true; it is possible that our tendency to under-estimate risk evolved because more realistic creatures died out when hardship or battle put them in competition with us. Why should our scientific theories not be subject to the same adaptive pressures, and seem true to us because it is useful for us to believe them, rather than because they are in fact true? That is after all what we tend to say about the scientific theories of our ancestors. Astrology and Ptolemaic cosmology, we say, survived for so long because belief in them was useful to the societies in which they flourished, rather than because they were true. It would seem to be special pleading to exempt our modern sciences from this mode of explanation. But in that case, a view that relies on science alone to achieve knowledge will undermine itself: on its own terms, it is unlikely to be true. Our scientific theories are far more likely to approach truth if we have been designed by an all-good and all-wise Being who has given us intellectual capacities that are meant, over time, to develop a correct understanding of the universe. So, odd as it may seem, we have more reason to believe that scientific theories are largely true if nature has been created by a God than if science, itself, told us the whole story about nature.

I would submit one small amendment to this argument. Plantinga says that evolutionary theory allows for our everyday sensory beliefs, as well as our scientific theories, to be false. That can't be right: if our everyday beliefs about our environment are adaptive, they can't for the most part be untrue. We *must* get our everyday environment right, on the whole, else we would quickly die out. What we see and hear and touch provides information we need in order to find adequate food and shelter and avoid danger. We can't get that wrong on a regular basis and survive. Our more elaborate *theories* about reality are not subject to these pressures, however, and we have indeed survived quite well, over many centuries, with theories that were wildly wrong. This point applies to evolution by natural selection as much as any other theory, however, so Plantinga remains right that that theory, when taken as the whole truth about nature, tends to undermine itself. Science in general, including the theory of evolution, seems far more likely to be true if our minds have been designed by God than if they have arisen from a series of arbitrary accidents.

This argument gives believers less than one might think, however. It shows at most that science gains credibility when understood within a framework that includes a God, not that it is impossible otherwise; it leaves widely open what sort of God would be necessary to make sense of science; and one of the things it thereby leaves open is whether the God in question need resemble the God of any traditional religion. It is nice to have in hand some scientifically-relevant reason to favor belief in God, but this is not enough to justify a commitment to Judaism, Christianity, or Islam. And I cannot imagine that anyone actually does adhere to these religions on the basis of such an argument. We will do best to treat Plantinga's argument merely as a supplement to other reasons we have to believe in God, not a primary reason for such belief.

When we turn to the traditional religions in which belief in God is usually enmeshed, we find that the attempt of the new religious rationalists to wrest respect for their beliefs from modern science is more of a hindrance than a help. I have in mind in particular their willingness to countenance much factual falsehood in sacred texts while insisting that a few claims, central to their faith, may still be true. Is it really plausible that God would reveal His/Her true nature or will for human beings in a book riddled with falsehoods, from which we have to gingerly pick out the few nuggets of truth? The new religious rationalists want to show their respect for science by granting that Joshua did not stop the sun, that there never were people who lived for eight or nine hundred years, and that much of the magic attributed to Jesus probably did not happen—while still insisting that Jesus was resurrected (they are almost all Christians; for a Jew, the equivalent claim would be that there was a revelation at Sinai); historians who say otherwise, they suggest, are expressing an anti-religious bias. I concede that historians have failed to show—how could they?—that Jesus was *not* resurrected, or that there was no revelation at Sinai. But the fact that these events are recorded by writers who got so much else wrong should give us pause. Why suppose that the Biblical writers are right about these events if they lied or were mistaken about Joshua's stopping the sun, Jesus' magic, and a host of other things? Modern historians doubt that there ever was a mass enslavement of Israelites in Egypt, let alone an exodus of the sort described in the Bible. If none of these events occurred, it takes an enormous suspension of disbelief to suppose that anything remotely like the Sinaitic revelation occurred.

As a Jew, this example is particularly important to me: very little of my religion remains if truth in religion depends on historical accuracy and the story of Sinai is inaccurate. Some Christian writers have suggested that their religion is in better shape, since the only historical fact that matters to it is the resurrection of Jesus, and that is more easily insulated from historical refutation than an event that is said to have happened to an entire people. But Jesus explicitly describes himself as the heir to and fulfillment of Moses' teachings. So if Judaism is undone by history, Christianity will be as well. (Moses Mendelssohn, an eighteenth-century Jewish philosopher, famously responded to the suggestion that he convert to Christianity by saying that that was like telling someone who lived on the bottom floor of a house with shaky foundations that he should move to the top floor instead.) So will Islam. It might be hard to imagine how historical evidence could refute the claim that Muhammad spoke to the angel Gibreel. But Muhammad presents his teaching as the heir and supplement to the teachings of Moses. So if the central Jewish story about revelation at Sinai is undermined, the Quran becomes implausible as well.

In short, the historical accuracy of any of the texts sacred to the Abrahamic religions is a weak peg on which to hang one's religious hat, even if anti-religious biases pervade the modern historical assault on these texts. Nor are other religions in better shape, in this regard. There are good historical reasons for supposing that stories of miracles everywhere tend to arise late, after a religion has already been founded, and then to spread within the relevant religious community without any serious effort to ascertain their truth. Some religions do not depend much on miracles. No fact of history could affect the truth or falsehood of the aphorisms in the *Tao te Ching*, for instance, although there are miraculous legends about its author (born of a virgin, among other things) that may once have lent credence to the book. But if these religions are immune to historical refutation, that is because they do not appeal to the sort of evidence that modern science, and historians informed by modern science, can assess. Whenever a religious community claims that its sacred texts are validated by historical events, modern archeology and linguistics and carbon-dating can be used to show that those events did not take place as described—and in every case thus far examined, the evidence does tell against those claims.

Fortunately, there are good reasons to set science and history aside, when assessing the truth of revealed texts. In the first place, as I've already noted, the idea of a God is the idea of a being that by definition cannot be either verified or falsified by scientific means. No observations or experiments would suffice to prove the existence of God, nor would any observations or experiments suffice to show that God does not exist. (Scientific evidence can similarly neither prove nor disprove the existence of a spiritual principle pervading the universe like the *tao*—or a claim, like the one central to Buddhism, that there is a way of grasping the nothingness of ourselves that will end all our suffering.) It follows that even if we met Jesus, saw the wonders attributed to him, and followed him around day and night, we could not determine whether or not he was God, and even if we heard a great voice proclaiming the Ten Commandments at Mount Sinai, we could not know that that voice was God's. At most, if we directly witnessed these events, we could conclude that there are remarkable powers in the universe of which science is unaware. We might conclude that something like the magic of the *Harry Potter* books or a *Marvel* comic was possible, for instance. But that would allow us to believe in figures like Dumbledore or Superman, not in a God who transcends all other powers, and is their creator or ruler. Worshipping a Dumbledore-like god would be idolatry, for a Jew or Christian or Muslim. That is however the only kind of god that empirical evidence, and the sciences based on such evidence, could ascertain.

By the same token, neither our own observations nor the sciences based on human observation can assure us that God is *not* speaking to us, at any time or by way of any book. For the same reasons that science cannot disprove the existence of God, it also cannot prove that the Torah or Quran does *not* come from God. Which is to say that what is true in these books, if they have a truth to tell, is not a scientific matter.

And in fact they do not present themselves as telling scientific truths. The massive Hebrew Bible has one brief opening chapter on the creation of the universe, and that chapter is highly poetic, and short on detail. Later, its characters rely here and there on a supposed knowledge of animal husbandry (Genesis 30:37–43) or magic (Exodus 7:9–13). But these are minor incidents, the Bible offers no theoretical account of the forces behind them, and they are irrelevant to its religious teachings. The detailed physical and biological theories that one can find in Plato and Aristotle have no counterpart in the Bible, even in its so-called "wisdom" books. The same is true of the Gospels and Quran, and yet more true of the Vedas and Upanishads, the *Tao te Ching*, and Confucius' *Analects*. These texts are all clearly intended to give us some kind of *ethical* guidance, and a view of God or of a metaphysical principle with which we should be aligned, rather than anything that might compete with science.

That is also how the religious traditions based on these texts have for the most part treated them. St. Augustine understands the Biblical story of creation as an allegory for Platonic philosophy (the "light" that is created before the sun is the light of wisdom), although he may well have also believed that it literally happened. Maimonides says that if the best science we have could show conclusively that there was no creation, we would have to reject the literal level of the Biblical story, and attribute to it just an allegorical meaning. As it is, he thinks, we must reject the literal level of all anthropomorphic characterizations of God in the Bible, and he devotes much of his *Guide for the Perplexed* to showing how these passages can be given an alternative meaning. Augustine and Maimonides are among the most important figures in their respective traditions, moreover, and although their philosophical views as a whole were sometimes controversial, their methods of reading sacred texts were not. The classical and medieval rabbis, and the fathers of the church, were given to radical reinterpretations of scripture, often reading into it a philosophical or mystical teaching that they felt revelation must contain, and always stressing the ethical or theological upshot of the texts rather than their historical accuracy. What makes the Gospels true for Augustine, and the Torah true for Maimonides, is a metaphysical view that transcends empirical facts—that indeed shows the ultimate unimportance of empirical facts. What makes these books true for other, more mystical Christian and Jewish figures is a different metaphysics. But for none of the great shapers of Christianity and Judaism and Islam—for practically no one before the modern era—is the truth of a sacred text supposed to be like the truths of empirical science.

So what does "truth" mean, when it does not mean scientific truth? We might begin an answer to that question with the way "true," or the word generally translated as "true" (*emet*), functions in the Hebrew Bible. Most of the time, it characterizes a *person* or a way of acting rather than a sentence. The first time it appears is when the servant of Abraham, who has been looking for a bride for Isaac, tells Rebecca's father and brother that he has been led by God on a "true path" (*derekh emet*) to Rebecca; he then goes on to ask whether they will deal with him "in kindness and truth" by giving her to him (Genesis 24:48–49). Later, Jethro advises Moses to pick "people of truth" (*anshe emet*) to help him judge the people (Exodus 18:21; compare Nehemiah 7:2). We might translate *emet* as "reliable" or "trustworthy": a "true" person or path is a reliable or trustworthy one. (Jews call out in prayer, twice a day, "the Lord your God is true," which can only mean that God is reliable, someone whom we should trust.) That would bring the Hebrew word in line with some older uses of our English one. "Truth" in English is related to "troth"— as in, "I pledge my troth to you"—and to this day we think of a "truthful" person as one who does not simply utter accurate statements but is generally reliable, trustworthy.

Now sometimes the Hebrew Bible does use *emet* to characterize sentences. The Queen of Sheba exclaims, "True was the report I heard in my land about your words and your wisdom!" after Solomon satisfactorily answers her questions (I Kings 10:6). Deuteronomy requires that reports of idolatry in a city be carefully investigated, and acted on only if they turn out to be "true and certain" (Deuteronomy 13:15). This is close to the way we use the language of truth today: to assess sentences that can be checked by direct observation. But in the context of a book that uses "true" mostly to assess people and paths, its application to sentences is a derivative one. The question the Bible raises, when it employs the word *emet*, is, "Can you *trust* this person, path, or sentence?" And in the case of a sentence—or *certain* sentences: ones that raise suspicions, as the report of Solomon's wisdom did for the Queen of Sheba, and as reports of idolatrous cities should for all Israelites—the way to establish trust may require direct observation, or a mode of inquiry that foreshadows those of modern science. When it comes to trusting people or paths, no such observational test or method of inquiry may be available. Moses presumably picked his assistant judges by general assessments of character, and Abraham's servant could find only a *sign* that he was on a reliable path to Isaac's bride. In any case, the point of calling something "true" in the Bible seems clearly to be that one can rely on it, not that it has survived the tribunal of logic or empirical evidence. A person or path of truth, and perhaps even a true sentence, is one that we can and should *trust*, whether or not he or it has passed logical or empirical tests.

When we ask whether the Hebrew Bible itself is true, then, we should realize that in its own terms that question means "Can and should we *rely* on it? Does it provide a trustworthy guide to our lives?" And this question is very different from the question, "Do its statements check out, empirically? Does it pass the tests we have devised to match it up with our own observations?" Once again, in its own terms, the Bible thus seems to avoid being treated like an object of scientific investigation. It calls on us instead to trust it for guidance, to establish some kind of ethical relationship to it.

In addition, our discussion of truth in the Bible shows that at least one ancient culture treated truth quite differently from the way we do in our modern, scientifically-dominated age. We have seen also that the Bible's use of truth language had analogies in some aspects of earlier English usage; I believe that there are similar phenomena in many pre-modern societies.

In any case, we now have in hand a model for understanding truth that takes us away from the idea that science provides the sole touchstone for whether claims merit that designation. Let's develop this model a bit; I think we'll find that it captures many of our intuitions about truth, which we suppress when we think of it in scientific terms alone.

Start with the thought that truth primarily applies to speakers, rather than what they say, and that it calls on us primarily to *trust* what they say—to follow it even when we cannot check or test it for ourselves. Is this claim about truth itself true? Well, think about the occasions on which we find ourselves needing the word "true." If you say to me, "There's a black squirrel on that tree," while we are both looking at it, I *may* say, "That's true," but I may also just nod, or repeat what you said—"Yes, I see the black squirrel," or, to a friend near us, "Look, there's a black squirrel." In general, when I understand what you say and have checked it out myself, I have no need of truth language: I can just affirm your reports. Things are sharply different if you utter a mathematical claim I don't understand, or tell me about something I haven't observed. Then I might well ask, "Is that true?"—of you or someone else—and seek some sort of assurance that I can rely on what you said. We characteristically ask after the truth of claims we cannot check ourselves, and want some reason to trust anyway. We wonder about a scientific theory that we don't understand well, or about a scientific claim based on experiments that others have carried out. So we ask a scientist who knows the field whether it is true. We wonder about a mathematical or logical sentence but do not have the skills to investigate it for ourselves. So we ask a mathematician or logician whether it is true. Or we wonder whether morality, or our religion, requires a particular action of us. So we ask someone with greater wisdom, or knowledge of our religion, whether it is true that we ought to act this way. We may also ask others whether the person we have picked—for scientific or mathematical or moral or religious guidance—is truly knowledgeable or wise, or truly knowledgeable or wise in the respect that matters to us.

These are very different reasons for trusting and seeking guidance, but they all connect trustworthiness to truth. I suggest that in general we rely most on the language of truth when we are trying to figure out what we ought to believe or do, and want a trustworthy guide to help us figure this out. What concerns us in the first instance, in these cases, is whether our purported guide is truth*ful* or not; whether the particular claims he or she endorses are true or not will, we hope, follow from that determination. Now in science or mathematics, this sort of truthfulness can be ascertained fairly definitively. There are rigorous ways of checking the claims of our guides, which we expect them to know and use, and which we can ask others to use, if we suspect our guides of dishonesty. In religion and morality, there are no such rigorous tests. There is no way of checking definitively whether abortion is right or wrong, much less whether God really spoke on Sinai or whether that entails that one may not drive on the Sabbath. Certainly, there is no way of checking these things that is as formalized, or delivers as clear-cut answers, as the methods of proof available to logicians and mathematicians, or the ways of gathering and assessing evidence available to a physicist. But that does not mean that something different in kind is going on when we use the label "true" for the words of a priest or rabbi rather than a physicist. In both cases, we are trying to figure out whether a person's speech is trustworthy; the only difference is the criteria on which we base that trust.

I've used the word "guide" thus far for the people we are inclined to trust. More commonly, we call these people "authorities": we use truth language when we feel we need to trust scientific and mathematical and religious authorities rather than relying on our own observations and reasoning power. I'd like now to introduce a distinction between two kinds of authority. One kind I'll call "experts," while reserving the word "authorities" for the other. We turn to scientific and mathematical experts when we can't assess a factual claim on our own, and their expertise is constituted by their having gone through a training in the ways by which claims are checked in their particular field. The marks of their expertise, then—their degrees, academic position, or whatever—are supposed to assure us that they know the proper way of checking claims in their field, and use it with integrity. Their credentials give us confidence that their ability to check these things can stand in for our own; in turning to them, it is *as though* we checked the claims ourselves. Which is to say, we regard experts as in principle on the same epistemic level with ourselves, who have simply invested their energy in acquiring skills that we have not acquired. Just as we might turn to a trained shoemaker to make our shoes, although in principle we could have learned to make shoes ourselves, so we turn to a scientific expert to verify factual claims that we have not learned how to verify. Of course it is possible that we are incapable of acquiring the intellectual skills by which scientists do their work, but even then we see them as people who have extended the capacities for observation and reasoning that we ourselves possess. We do not see them as morally or spiritually superior to ourselves; we regard them as our moral equals, and don't look to them to change our ideals or orientation in life. In short, we employ experts when we know what we want to do and simply need information that will help us do it, not when we are trying to figure out what we should be doing in the first place—what our aims, overall, ought to be.

Things are very different when it comes to ethical and religious authorities. There we are often looking precisely for someone we can trust to help us figure out what we should seek overall—and perhaps to help change us so that we desire the new ends they help us set. There, also, we don't expect that we will have any clear way of testing our guides—the very notion of "testing" them suggests a position of superior wisdom that, by hypothesis, we don't think we occupy—nor do we suppose that there is any clear method of training them to ensure that their claims are accurate. In selecting a guide, we look for some general virtues—integrity, humility, sensitivity—as well, perhaps, as some assurance that they share our overall ethical or religious orientation. We look for *signs* that they can lead us on a good path, as Abraham's servant looked for signs that Rebecca was the person God wanted him to choose as a bride for Isaac, or as Moses looked for signs that his assistant judges were *anshe emet*: people of truth or integrity. And we are far more concerned that they are truthful speakers, on the whole, than that any particular thing they say is true. We are not employing them, as we employ scientific experts, to help us attain a purpose we have already set by ourselves, but to help us set those purposes in the first place—to help us determine what kind of life we should lead. In this context, it can even happen that a truthful (trustworthy) authority may appropriately say something to us that, taken literally, is *false*.

An example: The wise and honest Aloysius tells me that I will find a great treasure in the village over the mountain. Greedy fellow that I am, I dash off to look for it. But what I actually find is a terrible famine. Having brought along a lot of food to keep me going while I looked for the treasure, I am in a position to alleviate the suffering, and set to work doing that. As it happens, alleviating suffering has a powerful impact on me, so I come back from the village feeling rather good about life. I am, however, still annoyed that there was no treasure. When I tax Aloysius with this, I become even more annoyed, because it turns out that he knew perfectly well that people were starving in the village, and there was nothing for me to acquire. "But," he says, "the opportunity for you to help others—and to discover the joy of doing that—was that not a great treasure?" If I agree that it was, as I might, I will surely not regard Aloysius as a liar. If I also ruefully acknowledge, as I might, that I would never have gone to the village had Aloysius not used the word "treasure," I may even admit that he told me the truth—in the only way I could then have heard it.

This story resembles the folktales of many pre-modern traditions, where the idea of following a guide in life—a guru, a prophet, a sage—was far more common than it is today. We put too much stock today in individual autonomy to be comfortable with these sorts of guidance relations. That is perhaps why the very idea of an ethical authority, and the kinds of truth-telling associated with it, have become unfamiliar to us. But even today many of us do take ethical guidance from various figures, and in any case we retain enough pre-modern folktales that we can recognize what an authority looks like. As I will explain shortly, such authority is essential to revealed religion.

Meanwhile, note three features of my story:

First, I would not regard Aloysius as truthful—honest—if he regularly misled me. It is only if his own path of life is a decent and thoughtful one, and if he employs the style of indirect advice exemplified by this story only in circumstances in which it is clearly necessary to lead his listener to a better life, that anyone would grant that this advice is part and parcel of truthfulness, rather than a violation of it.

Second, Aloysius's choice of words are tailored to the particular characteristics, including the particular vices, of his listener; what he says would be flatly false if directed to someone with different traits.

Third, the idea that the sentence, "There is a treasure in the village over the mountains" may in the end be true depends on its being given a particular interpretation, and on that interpretation making sense to its recipient only after he has changed how he lives. Moreover, the sentence shifts its register as it gets reinterpreted. At first, it looks like it concerns "treasure" in the literal sense of that term; later, the word turns out to be metaphorical, or at least to take on a new literal meaning, different from the one that the recipient expected.

Ethical authorities generally display these three features. We trust such authorities, when we do, only if their general conduct of life shows integrity and ethical wisdom, and the occasions in which they seem to mislead can be readily explained as having been meant to help the person to whom they were addressed. We also can gain only from authorities who pay close attention to the particular characteristics of everyone they address, recognizing that what moves one human being will often be different from what moves someone else. And finally, following an authority makes best sense if one is carrying out an extended course of action and can periodically reinterpret what the authority says as one goes along. If the point is precisely to *transform* oneself, radically to change one's character or orientation in life, then that is likely to take a while, and to lead one to have a new, deeper understanding of what one's authority says after the change than one did before. This last point is the reason why authorities may employ obscure or indirect ways of saying things: what they want to convey cannot be properly understood by their listeners until those listeners have been transformed. And in the course of that transformation, the authority's utterances may well shift from a literal to a metaphorical register, or acquire new literal meanings that we did not expect them to have when we first heard them.

In sum, what we look for when we wonder whether we should trust a scientific claim—regard it as true—is very different from what we look for when we wonder whether to trust the words of an ethical authority. We use scientific evidence in the course of projects we have already determined for ourselves; we turn to ethical authorities to help us figure out what projects we should be pursuing in the first place. And revealed or sacred texts, I suggest, are best understood as ethical authorities. They are the words of an ethical guide, not a scientific expert, and that means that if they are true, they are true in the way that an ethical guide's words may be, not the way that an expert report may be true. All truth is trustworthiness (accuracy is just one mark or kind of trustworthiness). To call the Torah true means that one can trust it, and to call the theory of evolution true means that one can trust it. But there are different kinds of trust, and different reasons for trusting, and the reasons we have for trusting a person or a book to help us transform our lives are radically different from the reasons we have for trusting a scientific theory.

Consider, in this light, some of the main features of revealed or sacred texts. Like Aloysius' remark on treasure, the Torah and Quran and *Tao te Ching* are not straightforward: they are written instead in poetic, obscure language that cries out for endless interpretation. And as they are re-read over time, what they seem to be saying can shift enormously. The Torah acquired Platonic and Aristotelian and a variety of mystical meanings in late antiquity and the medieval period, as did the Gospels and the Quran;

in the modern world, Kantian and existentialist meanings have been found in these texts. Devout religious believers delight in this sort of interpretation and reinterpretation. The literal stories of the Torah are but its "garment," says one rabbi in the *Zohar* (a major source of Jewish mysticism), and "anyone [who] supposes that the Torah herself is this garment and nothing else, . . . will have no share in the world to come."

Again like Aloysius' remark on treasure, revealed or sacred texts appeal to different people in different ways. Some are moved by the moral content of these texts, some by the metaphysical insights that can be drawn from them, some by their poetry. Moreover, each text speaks to some types of people more than to others. (Later, we will see how this point helps underwrite an argument for religious pluralism: an all-good spiritual being might well have set things up so that some books reveal His/Her nature and will to some people, and other books to others, in accordance with the emotional and historical differences among us.) And we trust these books, when we do, because we think that they guide us morally and spiritually, give us wisdom about how to conduct our lives. When we wonder whether the sacred text we grew up with is true, or whether to convert to a tradition with a different sacred text, we look for signs of moral wisdom in the text, as Abraham's servant looked for moral signs that the bride he was considering for Isaac was really the person to whom God's "true path" was leading him. We do not test each sentence of the text for its literal truth the way we might the claims of a scientific theory. We do not even *understand* the text fully, and instead try to draw a set of practices from it in the hopes that following those practices will help us understand it better. Which is to say that books of this sort issue in a practical path, and require never-ending interpretation as we proceed along that path.

It is essential to a revealed or sacred text that it be poetic and obscure; it is essential that it issue in a practical path; it is essential that it speak to its readers and listeners in accordance with their emotional configurations and not just their reason; and it is essential that it be, or seem to be to its adherents, something that bespeaks high moral and spiritual wisdom. These are features of an ethical authority, and the speech of such authorities is rightly called "true" if there is good reason to trust it when one pursues a radical transformation of oneself, or of one's orientation in life—when one tries to discover different overall purposes, and not simply a better way of achieving the purposes one already has.

This is not to say that factual questions are irrelevant when seeking a path of transformation. If Aloysius regularly got the facts wrong, nobody would consider him wise. Wise people, whether in legends or in real life, generally have a good sense of practicalities, understand the natural and human world, and tailor their advice so that it fits in realistically with human nature. Religious teachings accordingly appear foolish if they insist on factual claims that are out of synch with what we know about physics or biology or human history. We also find it hard to put our trust in a religious teaching that flies in the face of what we take to be true metaphysically. I argued earlier that science can neither prove nor disprove the existence of God, but those confident that there is no God are unlikely to put their trust in the Torah or Quran. (Those confident that we have a real, substantial self are similarly unlikely to put their trust in Buddhist teachings.) And those convinced of God's existence by metaphysical arguments may feel they have added reason to trust a theistic revelation.

But these are *background* or *supplementary* reasons for trusting or not trusting a revelatory text; they cannot be our main reasons. Those who seek something like scientific truth in such texts—who complain of their obscurity, or try to assess them according to the canons of scientific expertise—have misconstrued what revelation is all about. If they want to assess the truth of these texts, they should instead be asking, "Does this text, when thoughtfully interpreted, offer an ethical wisdom we could not get without it?"

A negative answer to *this* question may be enough to reject a text's claim to revelation, and a negative answer may well be forthcoming as regards many such texts. But when we assess a text's claim to revelation on the basis of this question, whether positively or negatively, we are not concerned with its *factual* truth. The standard of truth (trustworthiness) that we bring to purportedly revealed texts is an ethical, not a scientific, one; ethics is the appropriate sphere in which to adjudicate the question of revelation. We turn to it in the next chapter.

2

Ethics

I argued in the previous chapter that sacred texts serve as ethical authorities for those of us who believe in them: we seek ethical guidance from
them. But to what extent can that be so? Many people suggest that the
Ten Commandments, or Jesus' admonition to love one's enemies, taught
the world moral truths it had not known before. We trust a person or
book as an ethical authority, however, only *because* she or it seems to
have integrity, and insight into moral questions; we use morality as a
criterion by which to *select* our authoritative texts and teachers. That
suggests that we bring an understanding of morality to the decision
about whether to trust a sacred text or not. People do not regard a
book as sacred if it seems to them evil.

So which is it? Do we learn what is good from our sacred texts or do we
bring a notion of goodness with us in coming to those texts? I will argue
in this chapter that we do both: that goodness must be in part independent of revelation but that we also look to revelation to teach us about
goodness. This two-sided moral relationship to sacred texts reflects a
two-sidedness in goodness itself. Consider our ordinary intuitions about
the word "good." We have no doubt that helping an elderly person across
the street is a good thing, and that it is good to care for our children and
refrain from violence. We may also say confidently that freedom and
happiness are good, and that finding someone to love is a great good. But
when asked what distinguishes a good life, overall, from a mediocre one,
we often find our confidence that we know what goodness is wavering,
and may begin to wonder whether there is some over-arching good—
being saved by Christ?, overcoming our attachment to ourselves?, uniting with one another in a property-less society?—that we might be
missing. And it is possible that such an overall good would upset our
ordinary intuitions about goodness. Perhaps our intuitions about the
goodness of, say, romantic love or the freedom of worship are themselves

not good? (Some religious people would say the first and some Marxists the second.) Perhaps they are instead dogmas that ought to be punctured, like the moral beliefs of sexist or racist societies? It can be very hard to answer challenges like this once they get started, and although we are likely to remain convinced that it is good to help our neighbors, and bad to manipulate or beat them, we may suddenly become aware that we are not sure how to defend even these intuitions—what reasons we might give for them that could fit into a systematic account of the good.

Socrates made people nervous by leading them to this sort of vertigo about their moral beliefs, and Plato used that vertigo to argue that the highest good radically transcends our ordinary beliefs about goodness. Their approach to this subject is still relevant today, moreover, and nowhere more so than among followers of revealed religions, to whom it is of fundamental importance that the ultimate human good cannot be found in our ordinary intuitions and reasoning, and must be sought instead in a text or teaching that has a supernatural source. Even they, however, usually share the confidence of their secular neighbors that kindness and fairness are good, and trust their favored text in large part because they think that the way of life it recommends can help them better achieve this ordinary goodness. So the term "good" seems riven between an ordinary sense in which it should be wholly accessible and another, extra-ordinary sense by which it can turn on its own ordinary uses and find them wanting. The account of goodness that I'll offer in this chapter will reflect this tension.

We begin with the aspect of goodness that must be independent of revelation: the secular aspect of goodness, as we might call it. It is of course simply untrue that human beings had to wait until the Torah proclaimed the Ten Commandments before they became aware that there was something wrong with murder, theft, or adultery. These and many other moral principles are widely shared, across cultures and religions, and one can explain what they entail, and find reasons for adhering to them, independently of religion. Without many of these principles, societies would fall apart. Practically all human beings realize this, and accordingly have reason to be morally good whether they are religious or not. Indeed religious people are not necessarily better, as regards everyday morality, than non-religious people. Sex scandals, fraud, and cruelty are notoriously to be found among priests and preachers as well as other people. The same temptations plague all of us, and there is no guarantee that religious commitment will protect us from them.

This is not even to mention the moral corruptions that religious commitment itself may breed. Religious wars, the oppression or murder of non-believers—these pathologies are to be found in almost all religions that have lasted for any length of time. In addition, the simplistic reward and punishment models by which many religious people claim to underwrite morality—if you're good, you'll go to heaven; if you're bad, you'll go to hell—work against proper moral motivation, encouraging in us the selfish concern for our own fate that morality is supposed to counteract, rather than a true love of our neighbors, or of virtue for its own sake. Who is more admirable, the person who is good out of fear of God, or the person who is good because she cares for the well-being of her friends and neighbors? Even the person who acts purely out of *love* of God, if she does not also love other human beings, has a less than ideal kind of motivation. It seems reasonable, indeed, that a truly good and loving God would want us to love one another and not just Him. But that means that there are religious as well as secular reasons to expect that we don't need religion to be good.

We also don't generally need religion to figure out what *is* good. To a large extent, our moral vocabulary is geared towards purely humanistic ends: we approve morally of what preserves peace in our societies, what enables us to respect one another, and what enables us to alleviate one another's suffering. To a correspondingly large extent, our motivations for being moral are humanistic: we act morally because we want to live in peace and friendship and mutual respect with our neighbors. No proclamations by Moses or Jesus or Muhammad are necessary for us to know what we ought to do in these respects, nor is a doctrine of heaven and hell needed to spur us into doing it.

Moreover, it is just as well, from a religious standpoint, that this be so. We want some criteria, independent of religious teachings, by which to ascertain which teachings might be divine, and one important criterion is whether they are morally good. When we call a text morally good, we don't mean that it is good *by definition*: that it defines goodness and then lives up to its own standards. No, we are presupposing a notion of goodness independent of the text and saying that it does well by that standard. Our ordinary, humanistic moral vocabulary provides us with this independent notion of goodness. We can recognize that a religious teaching gives us great moral insight into ordinary human affairs—into the best way to express compassion, say, or settle a dispute—even before we grasp or accept the rest of its teaching. That assures us that when we call our favored teaching "good," even a supreme *fount* of goodness, we are not uttering a tautology.

An independent, humanistic notion of goodness also has religious value in another way. We need to interpret our religious texts—no text is self-interpreting, after all, and religious texts tend to be more obscure than others—especially if we want to draw a way of living from them. Notoriously, there are more and less humane ways of doing this, and an independent sense of goodness can guide us toward the more humane ways. An independent notion of goodness can, that is, help keep us away from religious pathologies. And surely an all-good God, who loves His creatures, would want us to understand His word in as humane a way as possible: to be led by it to a generous and fair way of dealing with one another. So an all-good God will presumably want us to interpret any revelation He gives us in accordance with an independent, humanistic standard of goodness. We'll come back to this idea in Chapter 6.

Finally, sacred or revealed texts tend themselves to make clear that they pre-suppose an independent notion of morality. When Genesis reports that the people of Noah's generation were "corrupt" and "violent" (Genesis 6:11), it assumes that the reader already knows what these terms mean, and why corruption and violence merit punishment. Later, Genesis takes for granted that its readers will see what is wrong with the dishonesty of Jacob and the brutality of Joseph's brothers, and Exodus makes no sense unless the reader recognizes that Pharaoh's oppression of the Israelites was unjust and cruel. The reader of the Gospels is similarly supposed to see Jesus' personal behavior as noble, and his admonition to love those who hate you as a moral improvement over the more judgmental doctrines that he attributes to his predecessors. The Upanishads presume that their readers see the evil in petty selfishness, and seek a way of overcoming it, and the Buddha acquired his first followers as much as anything by the "middle path" of virtue he proclaimed, which purported to improve on Hindu practice by eschewing both luxury and asceticism. In all these cases and many more, religious teachings presuppose that their followers are able to see something admirable in them as measured by an independent sense of morality: presuppose an independent moral understanding that helps us see them as the words of God, or of a supremely wise teacher. Religious texts themselves allow the humanistic, everyday sense of goodness that religious and secular people share to serve as a criterion for their trustworthiness. If goodness can have specifically religious features, they imply, these must be grafted on to a prior, humanistic base.

Now, some may complain that I have thus far made the process of grounding a humanistic morality, and laying out its demands, look too easy. They may for instance emphasize our many moral disputes. Some think that there is nothing wrong with abortion; others consider it tantamount to murder. Some regard capital punishment as a great evil; others think that morality *demands* capital punishment for certain crimes. We disagree similarly over homosexuality, government aid for the poor, and the circumstances, if any, in which war is justified. These disagreements pervade even societies that largely share language, history and religion; differences across cultures can get yet sharper. So surely it is a mistake, far too simple at any rate, to suppose that our reason or feelings or need to share a society leads us to converge on moral norms—even *if* we all agree in general that murder and fraud and cruelty are wrong, and that it is a good thing to be honest and courageous. Surely, indeed, it has been the project of moral philosophers to try to come up with principles that would *enable* us to share a detailed morality, to bridge the differences we have over abortion, capital punishment and the like. What good are utilitarian and Kantian principles if they can't help us resolve moral differences?

Well, in fact, utilitarianism and Kantianism, and the other systems promoted by moral philosophers, do not resolve our moral differences. In part, this is because they disagree with one another, and in part it's because they are too general to resolve most concrete disputes. Utilitarians ask us to consider which of two actions or policies will bring the greatest happiness to the greatest number of people. But happiness is hard to measure, and the consequences of most actions and policies hard to predict. So the implications of utilitarianism for disputed issues are unclear, and people who come to the issues with different predilections can easily load their description of the facts in question to get the result they want. Kant's categorical imperative asks us whether we can will that everyone take the type of action we are considering, or whether that action is compatible with respect for other human beings as ends in themselves. But these questions employ such abstract terms that they can easily be interpreted to yield results on both sides of most disputed issues. As a result, there are utilitarians and Kantians on all sides of practically every issue: utilitarians who support capital punishment and utilitarians who oppose it, Kantians who support capital punishment and Kantians who oppose it, etc. Attempts to systematize morality tend merely to add yet another level of disagreement to our everyday ones: over what the correct justification ought to be even for positions on which we agree.

We might add that these systems focus on different aspects of our ideals and norms, and therefore speak past one another. Utilitarianism focuses on the fact that we all seek happiness, Kantianism on the fact that we seek freedom and dignity. Other moral philosophers emphasize the place of sentiment in moral life, as opposed to the stress that both utilitarians and Kantians place on reason and rules, or urge us to attend less to particular actions and more to general character traits, like courage and self-command. But we all want happiness as well as freedom as well as good character traits, and we all see good societies as in need of fair rules as well as emotional sensitivity. "Morality" is a word we use for ideals and norms that serve a variety of different needs, so it shouldn't be surprising if attempts to systematize these ideals and norms sometimes pull us in different directions.

It is worth noting that religiously-based moralities do no more to resolve our moral differences. Not only do different religions conflict with one another at least as sharply as different philosophical systems do, but *each* religion tends to divide over many moral issues. There are Christians who consider homosexuality a terrible sin, and Christians who think that gay love should be recognized in church weddings. There are pro-life and pro-choice Christians, Jews, and Buddhists, and Christians, Jews, and Buddhists who support capital punishment as well as Christians, Jews, and Buddhists who oppose it. And while there is a higher degree of moral consensus in small communities—among Satmar Hasidim, say, or Mennonites—even these communities notoriously argue among themselves over things like whether to report sexual predators to the secular authorities, or how to treat dissenters. Plato noted 2500 years ago that morality is the primary locus of disagreement among people, and no one before him or since has come up with a formula to overcome that disagreement. It is a fact of the moral life that we disagree sharply over many moral issues; any reasonable theory of morality has to make room for that disagreement.

But this fact goes together with the other one I have been stressing: that people who understand morality in very different ways nevertheless *agree*, much of the time, on how to assess moral situations. People in daily life converge more often than not on what counts as cruel or dishonest behavior, and when, on the contrary, someone is courageous or generous. The degree of agreement here can be very high. Neighbors with extremely different religious and political views nevertheless see eye to eye on which of their number is a delight or a jerk. People also agree across societies on general virtues—they condemn cruelty, dishonesty, and selfishness and praise their opposites—even if they sometimes interpret them differently.

What is striking about morality, then, is that we *both* agree *and* disagree about it. We agree on its general contours, and on many of its specific demands, but then disagree so sharply on some specific cases, and on the rationale for being moral, that we wonder how the agreement we do achieve is possible. A good theory of morality must account for both our agreement and our disagreement. I'll come back to this point shortly.

Consider first an additional source of moral disagreements. This derives from the second meaning of "good" I mentioned earlier: whatever it is that makes a human life good overall, which may in principle override our ordinary intuitions about goodness. If you think a good human life requires the acceptance of Jesus Christ as one's savior, you have one conception of the good human life; if you think the overall human good requires that one recognize Muhammad as the final and greatest prophet, you have a different conception. Alternatively, you might think that the highest human good consists in uniting one's particular self with a more comprehensive world-Self or, to the contrary, that our good requires us to understand that we have *no* self. These different views go with familiar differences in religion, but a similar diversity can be found among secular people. Over the past two centuries, many secular people have thought that the true or highest human happiness will be achieved only when we are bound together in a single, classless community. But others have thought that the freest or happiest human life can be found only if we embrace a radical individualism. There are also people who think that politics is of supreme importance to a good human life and people who think that it doesn't matter at all; people who think that art provides the highest realm of human achievement and people who scorn the very notion of "art;" people who place erotic love at the core of the human good and people who consider eros to be vastly overrated. These are deep and abiding differences, and they are ubiquitous, making for sharp distinctions among secular as well as religious people. Insofar as they affect morality, they make it difficult to see how we could ever overcome moral disagreement.

Do they affect morality? Well, in one sense they must. One of the main meanings of the adjective "good" is that a thing promotes a goal of importance to us, and the noun "good" often denotes something we regard as such a goal. Utilitarianism is based entirely on this goal-oriented use of "good," and even moral systems that stress the sense in which "good" characterizes a way of acting regardless of one's goals ("it's good to tell the truth even if you don't get what you want that way") have to acknowledge that our overall goals in life are also goods, and whatever promotes them must have something good about it. If we have an ultimate goal, therefore, it can't but affect what actions we approve of. If I consider the ultimate good in life to be accepting Jesus as my personal savior, that will have to affect how I act. Indeed, as we'll see in the next chapter, ultimate goals like this one tend to organize much of our activity, and one reason we are concerned to identify them is so *that* we can figure out how to organize our lives. In any case, Christians and Muslims, communists and nationalists, and devotees of art or eros all *do* tend to organize their lives around their ultimate goals, and to approve of an action as good to a large extent on the basis of how well it serves these goals.

But at the same time we have a remarkable ability to abstract from our ultimate goals when considering whether or not a particular action is immoral, or whether or not a particular person has decent character traits. Christians and Muslims, communists and nationalists, and people with very different views on the importance of love or art will agree in most cases on what counts as a lie or a mean-spirited person, or on the other hand as an act of kindness or a courageous person—and agree in condemning the former and praising the latter. They agree, that is, on particular acts and character traits even though they disagree about the goals of life overall. They are able to set aside their differences on how to live, overall, and share a large number of ideals and norms.

I propose from now on to reserve the word "morality" for the ideals and norms on which we can agree despite differences about our overall goals, and use the word "ethics" for the broader values that include, in addition to morality, the religious, cultural, and aesthetic commitments by which we determine how to live overall. I'll also refer to the question about how to live overall as "the telic question"—from the Greek word "telos," which has traditionally been used in philosophy for the overall goal or purpose of a thing—and call our answers to it, "telic views." Telic views will then be part of ethics but not part of morality, and our judgments about whether a certain action or way of living is admirable or contemptible, inspiring or deadening, will also often be ethical rather than moral ones. All moral judgments will be ethical ones—ethics includes morality—but not all ethical judgments will be moral ones.

This terminology enables us to keep track of what we agree on and what we don't, as regards goodness. It also tracks our intuitive response to questions like "Is he a good person?," when asked about someone we consider honest and kind but committed to religious or political projects of which we disapprove. We are likely to say, in such cases, "Well, if you're asking about how he treats his family or co-workers, then yes, he's a good person, but I don't think his basic goals in life are good." We may for instance regard him as morally good but boring, shallow, or spiritually empty. On the other hand, we may sing the praises of a person as fascinating, deep, or exciting without meaning to call her morally good. One symptom of the difference between moral and telic evaluation is that we tend to get *angry* at people or actions we consider immoral, but merely sad or disappointed about people whose lives strike us as empty or misguided. The anger that comes with morality reflects a sense that the people we are criticizing already agree to the grounds on which we criticize them; we feel we are holding them up to their own norms and ideals. Not so for telic values—there we at best hope to persuade others, one day, to share our views. Anger at their not doing so now is consequently out of place.

Religious, aesthetic, and cultural values thus stand somewhat outside morality, although they use words like "good" and "bad" in a related sense: both telic and moral values pertain to how we think human beings most admirably conduct their lives. Someone might therefore want to insist that *anything* that bears on how we should live is a moral concern—those with the wrong religion, or who fail to appreciate art, cannot be good people. But it seems to me this is a less natural way of using our evaluative vocabulary than the one I propose, and even someone who insists on it is likely to concede that the issues to which our non-controversial norms and ideals are relevant—murder and rape, or on the other hand treating others respectfully and helping those in need—are the *core* of what we mean by "morality."

At any rate, with our terminological distinction in hand, we can propose a simple solution to our conundrum about why we both agree and disagree on what is good: we agree on moral goodness so that we can continue to *dis*agree on telic goodness. That is, morality preserves our ability to live in a society in which we can freely and peacefully pursue our different ideas of how to live overall. We can't be religious Jews or Christians, or discuss and pursue communist or libertarian ideals, or create or appreciate any art, if we live entirely alone. We can't do any of these things if we are oppressed or manipulated by our neighbors either, and we are unlikely to have the psychological strength to pursue our various ideals if we are constantly humiliated. So to pursue any telic view at all, we need norms that will allow us to live together in society, and we can best do so in a certain kind of society: a peaceful one that also co-operates against natural dangers, allows its members individual freedom, and encourages mutual respect among them despite their differences. It is the need for these things that gives rise to morality, and the wide agreement that prevails over it. The importance of morality to our ability to *disagree* on ethics is one reason why we agree on it, and get so angry if it is violated. About morality but not ethics overall, we can reasonably say to others, "You need these norms as much as I do; you *must* heed them, if you and I are to be able to disagree peacefully on other things, including those that matter most to us."

Now, one might object that the view of morality I'm giving is geared to liberal societies, and that before the rise of liberalism in the seventeenth and eighteenth centuries, there were many societies that did not distinguish between norms that maintain society itself and norms that promote a good life overall. There is some truth to this objection, but the distinction I am emphasizing is not restricted to modern societies. The idea that compulsion is not the proper way to bring someone to a religious tradition has long been embedded in mainstream Judaism, Christianity, and Islam, despite the history of forced conversion to which the latter two have been prone; the ancient Buddhist emperor,

Ashoka, included a similar principle in his rock edicts. Accordingly, all these traditions and many others contain important strands suggesting that law should enforce just the principles necessary for society to provide its members with peace and basic dignity. The medieval Christian philosopher Thomas Aquinas, for instance, declared that human laws cannot and should not "forbid all vices from which the virtuous abstain, but only the more grievous vices from which it is possible for the majority to abstain; and chiefly those that are to the hurt of others, without the prohibition of which societies could not be maintained: . . . murder, theft, and suchlike." Of course, Aquinas uses the word "virtue" for much that lies outside the reach of human *law*, but in drawing a distinction like this, he tacitly acknowledges that those aspects of morality to which everybody agrees, and which are necessary to society, are different in kind from the aspects to which one can merely hope to win others' assent over time.

In short, if the definition of "morality" I am urging is particularly characteristic of modern, liberal societies, it is so because modern, liberal societies have further developed a feature of moral judgment already present in their predecessors. Moreover, they have developed this feature because they understand better than their predecessors the depth of our disagreements over how life should be led overall, and the need, therefore, for each of us to come to our answer to that ultimate question on our own. I think we can reasonably regard the greater emphasis on freedom in the modern world as a moral *discovery*, that is, not an invention—something that improves our societies, and could have been recognized as such by our predecessors. In any case, this emphasis on freedom is essential to the way the word "morality," and its affiliated terms "good," "bad," "right," and "wrong," have come to be used. That is enough reason to maintain the distinction I have proposed between the moral and the telic, and to reserve "ethics" rather than "morality" for systems that encompass both morality and a telic vision.

But even within morality, as I have now siphoned it off from ethics, we will encounter fierce moral debates: over such things as abortion and capital punishment, or when, if ever, lying is permissible. How to settle these debates? Here the response of many moral philosophers over the past two centuries has been to offer a principle that is supposed to tell us the right thing to do in every circumstance. That, once again, was the hope of many utilitarians and Kantians, at least. It is widely agreed today that these projects have failed, that neither utilitarianism nor Kantianism yields unequivocal answers to most moral controversies, and that there is no clear way of deciding which system is right when they conflict. They remain of abiding interest because of their views of life as a *whole*—as aiming at happiness, on the one hand, or the expression of our freedom, on the other. But that, in my terms, places them in the realm of ethics rather than morality: puts them on equal footing with the religious, cultural, and aesthetic views that exacerbate rather than resolving our differences over the good.

In recent years, there has been a move among moral philosophers to look for procedures, rather than principles, from which uncontroversial moral norms could be generated. Some have proposed that morality should be *defined* as consisting just of those norms that would be accepted by people willing to agree on any norms at all. This is an appealing idea, but my own procedural proposal is a bit different. I think that we do, and should, include a norm under the rubric of morality in accordance with the degree to which we can defend it from the perspective of each of the different moral systems that have currency in our society. We try to defend the moral claims we make by appealing to widely accepted intuitions *and* utilitarian *and* Kantian *and* virtue-ethical concerns. This reflects the different ends that we want moral codes to serve. We can be confident that a particular action is moral only when we are persuaded that it promotes both happiness and freedom, expresses or cultivates admirable character traits, and fits in with our long-standing moral traditions to boot. Moreover, we rarely know exactly how to weigh these various concerns against one another, and are aware that our different telic views lead us to different ways of prioritizing them. Consequently, we best preserve our chances to pursue our own telic views, and best respect other people's right to pursue theirs, by arguing for our moral claims on as many different shared grounds as possible. This suggests that the agreement underwriting morality is and should be an agreement to rely on *eclectic* forms of moral argument, to address one another in terms of as many of the types of grounds we expect them to share with us as we can.

It follows that in a large and diverse society, there will be little room to appeal to religious arguments in defense of moral claims, while there may be more room for that in small, relatively homogeneous communities. It makes no sense for me to be angry at you—to regard you as immoral—for failing to follow the norms of my religion unless you share it. Consequently, I will appeal to my religion only when speaking to fellow members of my religious community—and will be aware, if I live, on the whole, in a larger and more diverse community, that what I call "good" to my co-religionists is not so in a purely moral sense. Even those who claim that their morality is derived from their religion tend in practice to recognize that it cannot be purely based on that if it is to command the allegiance of all human beings. Consider the way religious opponents of abortion argue for their position. They may cite Scriptural verses, but most of the time they instead produce pictures designed to arouse horror at abortions or to help us see the fetus as human. Alternatively, they appeal to analogies with slavery or the Holocaust to suggest that ignoring the humanity of the fetus is like ignoring the humanity of black people or Jews. Sometimes they add claims about the need for a universal prohibition on the taking of life or assert that abortion harms the women who have them. They appeal, that is, to emotivist, intuitionist, Kantian and utilitarian conceptions of morality: they appeal to *secular* moral systems. And while they may do this in part because, in liberal democracies, it is problematic to offer a purely religious basis for law, they also use these sorts of arguments among themselves, as part of their case for the claim that abortion is wrong in the eyes of God. De facto, then, they recognize the secular cast of moral discourse, and rely on it even in their reading of their religious sources. De facto, they recognize that religious appeals, to count as part of morality, must be grafted onto other kinds of moral reasons. A claim based on a scripture only becomes a moral claim—something we can expect anyone to heed, and blame anyone for dismissing—when we can show that it promotes general human welfare, protects individual freedom or dignity, or enhances virtues like courage and generosity. For religious arguments to be moral arguments, they need to be endorsed by the secular strands in our discourse, the strands on which people agree across all religions and none.

I think that this eclectic, fundamentally secular view of morality is correct both descriptively and normatively. We tend in fact to defend moral claims from many different, mostly secular perspectives, and this is also a good thing. It is good because it enables people of different religious and other telic views to live together in peace, freedom, and mutual respect. It is also good from the perspective of our various telic views because if just one of them dominated our moral discourse, those who held a different such view would find themselves despised or oppressed. Moreover, even the followers of the majority view would often be following it for the wrong reasons—out of a desire to conform, and without the critical perspective that would enable them to take it up thoughtfully, and correct it if necessary. In the past, certain religious views did dominate moral discourse in most societies, and that remains true in some places today. But the cost of that, to the liberty and dignity of dissenters, is high. An eclectic, mostly secular morality is best suited to a liberal society, and a liberal society has great moral advantages over societies that press everyone to conform to a particular religious view. The same goes for societies, like the former Communist nations, that press everyone to conform to secular telic views.

We might add that religious and other telic views tend not to form coherent moral systems on their own. Rather, different believers in the same religious tradition have different views on concrete moral questions, and align themselves with different moral philosophies. There are Christian utilitarians and Christian Kantians, Christian virtue ethicists and Christian conventionalists, even some Christian rational egoists. The same goes for every other religious tradition. Consequently, religious appeals in moral argument can be contentious even within what at first seems a homogenous community. Many Christians would be upset if one kind of Christian morality were regarded as "the" moral voice of Christianity. Conservative Christians would be horrified if moral discourse were dominated by voices who insist that gay love is blessed by Christ, and liberal Christians would be just as horrified if conservative Christianity dominated moral discourse. Better, again, for all Christians (and Jews, Muslims, and other believers), if the voices entering into their society's moral consensus are mixed enough that each can find some support for the moral reading she is inclined to give of her religion.

In sum, we manage to uphold a joint morality in spite of our disagreements by agreeing to an eclectic way of arriving at moral conclusions that allows us, on many important issues, to continue to disagree. We agree to disagree—agree to a way of managing our disagreements that allows us to preserve our telic differences while still living together in peace, freedom, and dignity.

We can now return with more confidence to the position I floated at the beginning of this chapter: that morality, at least at its core, is independent of religious revelation. I want however to acknowledge that the line between what I have called "morality" and what I have called "ethics" is not sharp, and religious and other telic commitments can affect what we regard as morally good and bad. Consider a decision about whether to withdraw life-support from a relative whom doctors agree is unlikely to recover from a brain injury. Many people will be guided by their religious traditions on a question like this. Our various secular moral systems do not clearly tell us what to do in cases of this sort, and often pull in different directions. A utilitarian may be concerned about minimizing the sick person's suffering, for instance, while a Kantian may think that suffering is less important than the ability to make rational choices. Utilitarians and Kantians also disagree among themselves about such cases. Failing to get a clear or convincing secular answer to their conundrum, people with strong religious commitments often turn to their religious tradition for guidance. Similarly, even people who defend a pro-choice position as regards legal restrictions on abortion may look to a religious tradition for guidance as to whether they personally should have an abortion. Some other moral issues—attitudes towards eating meat, for instance, or pre-marital sex—tend also to be strongly affected by religious commitment.

Why these particular issues? Why is one more likely to seek a Jewish or Christian or Hindu principle when making choices about the end of life or meat-eating or sexuality than about keeping promises, or lying on one's tax return? Well, one feature shared by the issues I have listed is that their resolution tends to turn on what one considers most valuable about human life as a whole. This is obvious in beginning- and end-of-life issues. Whether or not one considers a fetus to be a person with a right to life turns greatly on whether one thinks that our right to life depends on our rationality, our ability to experience happiness, or our having a God-given soul; the point at which one considers a person's life properly over turns similarly on views of this sort. But what one thinks about the ethical importance of animals, and the legitimacy, therefore, of eating them, also turns on what one considers to be important about human beings (do human beings have a unique value or do we share what makes us valuable with other animals?). And the place of sexuality in most people's lives is so basic to their other projects, their happiness, and their relationships with others, that it is hard to say much about what it should look like without addressing the question of what their lives should look like overall. This is not true, or not usually true, of keeping a promise, or lying on a tax return.

But of course the possibility that the question about how to live overall can come into play on *some* moral issues suggests that it hovers in some sense over *all* moral deliberations: that it stands in the background at least, and can always be triggered by hard cases. I think this is right and what we should expect. Telic views give us reasons for caring about the societies that morality holds together, as well as reasons for the importance of morality independent of its value for maintaining society. They lead us to see certain virtues as helping us to attain nirvana, or express our love for Christ, or align ourselves with the *tao*, or further the communist cause. Accordingly, what matters about moral action for a Buddhist may be different from what matters about it for a Christian, which in turn is likely to differ from what a communist sees as good about it. In any case, what telic views add to morality tends to be not so much a distinctive set of norms as a distinctive *role* for moral norms in the ultimate or overall human good. The *content* of the Ten Commandments and the Sermon on the Mount may not be especially novel, from a moral point of view, but the idea that our basic moral laws or attitudes are enjoined upon us by the God Who redeemed us from slavery, or Who loves us regardless of our sins, sheds a new light on what the business of being moral is about. Here and elsewhere, telic views affect morality most deeply by re-framing it. The Torah and Gospels and Quran, and the views promoted by secular communists and individualists, all place morality in a telic context, give it a point, a function, that goes beyond the fact that it enables us to share peaceful and free societies. That new framing for morality will, however, inflect our way of coming to moral decisions, and sometimes, therefore, have a direct impact on those decisions.

So the line between morality and ethics is not sharp, although we try, and should try, to keep them apart most of the time. Goodness is radically two-sided, and we have reason *both* to keep its socially-oriented face independent of its telic face, *and* to try, in some arenas, to integrate these two things. The tension between them will be important in the next chapter.

I want to close this chapter by returning to the question of what might make a revealed teaching true. In the previous chapter I suggested that we call certain ethical guides "truthful," and their words "true," when we consider them trustworthy without being able to assess their advice until we have followed it. Where in the realm of ethics, as we have now construed it, might there be a fitting place for such guidance?

Well, we turn to guides in many moral situations. I often ask my wife for moral advice. Most of us have relationships that help us in this way, and most of us can probably recognize the possibility that we might be helped by a wise person like Aloysius. But in all these cases, the fundamental ideals and norms by which we govern our actions are ones we think we could come to on our own, and which wholly secular views like utilitarianism and Kantianism can account for quite well. There is therefore no *essential* place for trust in a guide here: there will be a need for that only if, like the recipient of Aloysius' advice, we are blinded by deep character flaws, or an anger or fear that prevents us from seeing our circumstances aright. The everyday, garden-variety morality that keeps society peaceful and free is not so hard to figure out—it *can't* be, if it is to function properly. Putting an unquestioning faith in the word of others is therefore something of which we are commonly leery, and rightly so. We can easily get manipulated that way, or become a passive cult follower rather than an autonomous person.

This leaves us with the possibility that there may be an appropriate role for this sort of trust in ethics, the wider sphere of which morality is a part. Perhaps our telic views—our views of what makes life worth living overall—require a trust or faith of this sort. To be sure, not all telic views require any such thing. Utilitarianism and Kantianism are telic views as well as moral ones, and for Kantians, especially, making one's decisions by one's own lights is essential to a worthwhile life. For them, and for many utilitarians as well, autonomy is not just a condition for taking moral responsibility but something of tremendous importance in itself. And modern ethical philosophers who have attempted to revive the ancient Greek emphasis on virtue tend to share this emphasis on autonomy: it is basic to the liberal outlook that dominates the modern world. Given that emphasis, it is indeed hard to see how we could possibly have reason, on matters that concern what our lives are about overall, to subordinate the promptings of our own reason or feelings to the words of a teacher, text, or tradition. Yes, in certain limited cases, we might accept on trust the advice of a wise friend or teacher about how to handle a love relationship or to educate our children; we might even go looking for a "treasure" in the village over the mountains. But on the whole we are suspicious of people who ask us to trust them, and avoid rather than run to ethical worldviews based on such trust. This is especially so if "we" are college-educated Americans or Europeans, raised on the strongly individualist ethos that has pervaded Western thought and literature for the past two-and-a-half centuries.

Nevertheless, there have been many ethical outlooks organized around trust in certain texts and teachers, and the possibility that they might be true—trustworthy—remains intelligible today. What it would take for them to be true, I suggest, is that the overall goal of our lives be ungraspable by our untutored senses and reason alone. Perhaps we need, on trust, to follow a certain discipline that will transform how we perceive or understand value, or perhaps the mere act of putting trust in a source outside ourselves, of humbling our ways of perceiving and understanding, is a necessary precondition for our being able to grasp our true or highest end. In any case, if our highest good, what gives worth to our lives overall, is inaccessible to us unless we trust a certain text or tradition, then that text or tradition is surely trust*worthy*: true. It is that possibility that I will explore in the rest of this book.

But the modern, liberal reasons for being wary of such a possibility should be borne in mind throughout this exploration. It seems to me clearly *intelligible* that our highest good could be accessible to us only if we trust a sacred text or tradition, and I will argue that that is in fact likely. But it is still a *dangerous* possibility. What if the text or tradition in which we trust calls on us to override our ordinary moral beliefs, or to give up all the ordinary joys that seemed to make life worthwhile before we fell under its sway? It could be terribly destructive or self-destructive for us to trust a telic view of this sort.

No one should, and practically no one does, put *blind* trust in a religious tradition, however. The kind of guidance that I am considering is not one that calls on us to abandon our capacity for reasoning— Aloysius' advisee had *reasons* to trust him—and one excellent reason to *dis*trust a religious tradition is that it violates one's basic understanding of morality. Telic views should graft onto moral ones. What is good for us overall should be morally good, and should indeed help us understand and achieve morality better than we did before. So if someone tells us that a certain teaching will help us see and achieve the overall point of life, but that teaching endorses horrible crimes, then we have all the evidence we need that we should *not* trust it: that it is not a true (trustworthy) vision of our good. People who commit terrorism to further their religion may not see themselves as witnessing against their religion's truth, but that is in fact what they achieve. We have no reason to trust a view of our highest good that clashes irremediably with our beliefs about everyday, moral goodness.

With this caveat in mind, we may say that revealed teachings about how to live can be true if and only if there is room in ethics for us to be guided to a radically unfamiliar view of what to value. And that is most likely to be the case if the ultimate or overall significance of our lives is somehow mysterious, not directly accessible to us when we reflect on our own. To make room for the notion of true revelation, we therefore need to figure out why we might see the value of life as mysterious, and why, if it is that, a religious text or tradition might be the best way to gain access to it. Why should trust—faith—in a book give us better access to the significance of our life than we can get via our own, independent reason? The next two chapters take up that question.

3

Our Overall Good

What does a good human life look like, overall? Perhaps we can set this question aside for moral purposes—perhaps we *have* to set it aside, if we are to achieve a peaceful and free society—but at some point, we need to answer it.

Or do we? Some people, including some philosophers, regard the question as silly. Life is not a game or a competitive sport, after all, with an endline to cross, or points to amass for our achievements. We just do various things, and there are no prizes at the end for how well we've done them. If "what does the good human life look like?" means something like "what is the purpose of life?," then perhaps the answer is "life has *no* purpose, and it's a mistake to look for such a thing." And "what is the meaning of life?" or "what makes life worth living?" may be no better. We might say to the first that life is not a symbol or piece of writing, that it should have a meaning, and to the second that it is not an object to be acquired, that it should have a worth. Plenty of philosophers would urge us to get over the temptation to ask these questions, taking them to be symptoms of a pointless anxiety rather than something that could possibly have a good answer. Stop asking the questions and you will find the peace of mind you are looking for, they say. Only a person on the verge of suicide takes such questions seriously; healthy people just *see* what's good in life, and need no more to carry out their activities. Our practice refutes our doubts, one might say: as long as we have freedom, some material security, and are not perpetrators or victims of gross immorality, we all have good lives, and know that as we live them.

But it is not true that the question about the good human life is one that only a person on the verge of suicide is likely to ask. On the contrary, all of us ask the question, implicitly or explicitly, when organizing our goals and projects. Consider how we make decisions about careers. Should I go for a high-paying job at a consulting firm, or should

I instead work for an NGO, or try to make it as a musician? I may go for the NGO because I think I should devote my life to helping others, or I may pursue the musical option because I think people care about their lives only if they express their creativity. Or, valuing the luxuries that an ample income can bring, I may plump for the high-paying job. Any of these ways of making my decision will draw on what I think worth doing in life—what, overall, I'm aiming for. And if I change my mind about that later on, I may look for a different career.

I'm also likely to draw on considerations about a worthwhile life in picking a spouse. Even a passionate erotic attachment won't lead to a lasting marriage if the two of us don't want the same sorts of things out of life—don't share religious or political commitments, or value art or family life in the same way. And again, if my views on subjects like these change radically, I may re-evaluate my marriage, and end it, or continue it only after arguments and therapy.

It goes without saying that considerations of this sort also have a huge impact on how we raise our children. How important is it for them to take music or dance lessons? Should they go to a religious school, or is it important, on the contrary, that they go to public school? Then there's the question of what we teach at home. We may refuse to indulge our children's desires for endless toys or fancy clothes, or require them to read certain things, or to volunteer for charitable organizations. We may also discourage them from hanging around with people whose lives we think are a waste—people who spend all day watching TV, say—even when we regard these people as honest and kind. Or we *don't* think that it's a waste to spend all day in front of the TV, because it doesn't much matter what one does with one's life, as long as one is honest and kind. But even that is a view about the worth or point of life: just one on which life has *no* worth or point, or gets whatever value it has subjectively, from our desires.

In making career and marital decisions, and raising our children, our beliefs about what makes for a worthwhile life come to the fore of our deliberations, but they also play a background role in everyday leisure decisions—should I try to improve myself by reading history and literary classics, or is it fine to read only trashy romances?—and in some of our political views: on what should be taught in schools, or government funding for the arts, or whether the state should recognize same-sex marriages. What is morally good and bad is not enough to resolve these issues. When I wonder whether to "improve myself" by studying history and literature, I am not asking whether I'll thereby become kinder or more honest. And those who consider it incumbent on the state to recognize same-sex marriages, or wrong for it to do that, usually come to that view in virtue of a belief that sharing one's life with an erotic partner is a basic element of a good human life, or that respecting the prohibitions of a religion or tradition is essential to a good life.

So questions about whether life has meaning or a point are always with us, not just when we are severely depressed, even if our responses to that question hover in the background of our decisions rather than appearing explicitly. Even those who say they've never thought about the question, or are upset or irritated by it, display views on it in their actions. They may display a view on which life has *no* meaning or point and, within the bounds of morality, it doesn't matter what one does. But that too is a view of the overall human good, an answer to the telic question.

Our answers to the telic question differ sharply. Secular people often regard those who commit their lives to prayer or religious ritual to be wasting their time, while religious people often have the same attitude towards those who seek what is worthwhile in art or secular philosophy. Religious people also differ among themselves about *which* religion, or what sort of religious devotion, is truly worthwhile, and secular people differ over whether politics or art or love, or a combination of these things, best makes for a worthwhile life. We do not agree on this matter nearly as much as we do on morality, although we may consider it rude to voice our disagreements. I am unlikely to *tell* someone who spends all day watching TV that she is wasting her life, but I may well think that, and in planning my own life I am forced to take a stance on her way of living. If I think that endless TV-watching is a perfectly fine way of living for *her*, why do I not consider it good enough for me? If I think that Buddhism is a perfectly fine religion for *you*, why do I not practice it? I will need views on these and other candidates for a good human life if I am to determine which candidate I myself favor, and such views inevitably entail a disapproval of the lives of some of my friends and acquaintances, even if I do not voice that disapproval.

One important difference among telic views is whether they are naturalistic or not. Some telic views closely track the desires we have by nature, while others put up a candidate for the good life radically at odds with our natural desires. When traditional Christians say we need salvation from sin, and traditional Jews or Hindus call for a certain detachment from our desires for food and sex, they are asking us to *break* from what we naturally want. Muslims, Buddhists, and Jains issue the same call, if in different language. Revealed religions present views of our telos that break with what we are likely to come up with by fulfilling the desires that feel natural to us. They call on us to renounce much of what our natural faculties lead us to want in favor of a goal whose value we will see, they say, only once we commit ourselves to them—once we transform ourselves in accordance with the path they hold out to us. We can, therefore, appreciate their vision of our telos only if we first put a certain trust or faith in that vision. No such thing is necessary, on the whole, to appreciate secular, naturalistic visions of our good.

Which brings us to a crucial point: the non-naturalistic accounts of our highest good held up by various religions are appealing to precisely those who worry that our lives as naturally led are not worth living. The possibility that our lives are empty and worthless is a fear that human beings have had for millennia. We find it in the Biblical book of Ecclesiastes, for instance. The fleetingness of pleasure, the weakness that age brings on, the fact that so much of our lives is repetitious and devoted simply to maintaining life itself—we keep ourselves alive today just so that we can do it again tomorrow—and of course the overwhelming horror of facing what all natural evidence suggests will be an eternity of non-existence: these things have been clear to people in all ages, and can easily make everything we do seem pointless, and the sense of value we experience when filled with joy or hope seem an illusion. Philosophy was indeed born in large part as an attempt to dispel this fear, to answer our worries about death and repetitiveness and the emptiness of pleasure; many ancient philosophers looked above all for an activity that can take us beyond everything fleeting and repetitive, either in this life or in another one. For Plato and Aristotle, that activity was philosophical knowledge. For others, it was the achievement of virtue, or the union of our individual selves with a higher self that governs, or underlies, the universe. These views made it possible to see nature as something we can love: something in which our lives have a point. Today, few philosophers find these views plausible. But that just brings out the degree to which we lack secular, purely naturalistic resources for a satisfying view of our telos.

That said, what are the most promising secular, naturalistic views of our telos? And what can be said on their behalf? If a major reason to turn to religious claims on this subject is a belief that non-religious ones fail, we need to start with the non-religious ones, and see how they fare.

I will sort them into two broad categories:

(1) In the first category are views on which a *particular sphere* of life makes everything else worthwhile. This comes out when a person says, "we're put on earth to help others," or "love makes the world go around." We may also think of those who see the creation and appreciation of art as the highest thing that humans do, or the growth of knowledge as what gives our species a reason to exist. Other people find these conceptions of the good preachy or elitist, but even they may place all their telic eggs in one basket, and measure people's lives by whether they raise healthy children, say, or have a successful career.

(2) A very different approach to the good human life is to see *all* the spheres of activity I've listed as worthwhile, and the good life overall to combine them—either because they fulfill the capacities of our nature that most demand fulfillment or because happiness consists in the varied pleasures they grant, and happiness is ultimately what we want. A variant on this view has it that a good life consists in getting as much pleasure, from whatever source, as possible, or in satisfying whatever preferences one sets for oneself. All these views locate the goodness of life in some *general* feature of what we do—realizing our natural capacities, achieving pleasure, satisfying our preferences—rather than in a particular activity.

Let's take these categories one by one. I shall not try to show that conceptions of the good that fall under them are *wrong*, merely that we cannot show them to be *right* any more easily than we can show that of various religious views. The point is to bring out the degree to which secular and religious views of the good are on a par with one another, as regards their grounding—the degree to which both secular and religious views, in this arena, depend on a non-rational faith. Even secular people tend to hold onto a goal for human life—working for social justice, finding a great love, creating or appreciating deep and lasting art—in the face of empirical evidence that it is either unattainable or not that wonderful, and tacitly or explicitly fall back on various metaphysical pictures, no more plausible than the pictures of a religious metaphysics, when their empirical claims are challenged. The idea in what follows is to sketch such challenges and the metaphysical response they evoke, indicating in the process how and why secular, naturalistic approaches to the good, in general, may be unsustainable.

It sounds noble when someone says that we're put on earth to help others, or to make the world a better a place. But can that really be enough to make a life worth living? Helping others usually means making sure that they have adequate food and shelter, protection against violence, and a job that allows them self-respect—that they have all the *conditions* under which one can live a free and pleasant life. But once one has all these things, one still has to worry about what to *do* with them. Suppose everybody had all these things; suppose that injustice, violence, and poverty no longer existed, and most of us were able to avoid grave disease and natural disaster. What then? Would the question about the worth of life not arise even more acutely? In the midst of urgent threats to life and liberty, we can set that question aside; once the urgency has passed, it comes roaring back. Saying that we are here to alleviate the suffering of others just pushes the question off for a while. In a wonderful *Peanuts* strip, one character says to another that we are put on earth to help others, only to be asked, "what are the others here for?"

Sometimes the "we're here to help others" view takes a more political form. We're here, some say, to transform our social and political institutions in such a way that everyone can experience the joys of freedom, communal solidarity, and mutual respect. Once all hierarchies based on class, race, or gender are destroyed, we will come together in a way that will change our very nature, from a selfish, individualist one to one that is directed at its core to the good of our species as a whole. Then we will see the purpose of life, or won't worry about questions like that: the very question may be a symptom of the self-centered, capitalist world we live in.

I suppose something like this could be true, but there is no evidence that it is. Large-scale attempts to create non-classist societies, from the Soviet Union to Vietnam and Cuba, have never led most of their members to love their lives—or even to feel much communal solidarity—and a sense that their nicely-ordered and materially-secure lives were drab and pointless has been a major force in the breakup of small egalitarian communes like Israel's kibbutzim. More generally, political utopias of all kinds have failed to redeem the promise of human transformation that inspired them. Neither Gandhi's simple, peaceful India living out the best of its ancient traditions, nor Sukarno's plan for Indonesia to lead a revitalized Third World, nor Herzl's liberal Jewish community that could help and inspire the entire Middle East have come to pass, and the states to which they did give rise have for the most part bitterly disappointed their idealistic founders. People passionate about the liberating potential of politics may say, after every such disappointment, that the program wasn't carried out right, and that sometime in the future they will try again and succeed. But after a while claims like this ring hollow, and begin to look like the faith that religious people put in the coming of a Messiah. The idea that political programs can so transform us that we won't even be tempted to ask anymore after our ultimate good stops looking like a naturalistic claim at all, something that empirical evidence might support or refute. It becomes instead an article of faith, in no better shape than the religious faiths that advocates of progressive politics tend to dismiss. One might support this article of faith with philosophical arguments to the effect that individuals are part of a larger group mind or spirit, and can only realize their potential when they identify with their society. These claims look much like the metaphysics of a traditional religion, however, and have no better empirical support. Not all progressivists make such metaphysical claims, but I submit that most rely on them implicitly, when they cling to a faith that identifying with others *must* give value to life, in the face of the strong evidence to the contrary.

So what about "love makes the world go round"? Could it be that our lives gain whatever ultimate value they have, or the greatest component of that value, from our love relationships? People who say things like this may be talking about all sorts of love, but the kind of love that seems most likely to be what above all we aim for, and to make up for other hardships we suffer, is of course erotic love. Especially when we first experience it, it seems to make everything else in our lives worthwhile. We feel that we want to share everything with our partners, and find everything we do with them enhanced by sexual union. The joy we take in each other seems intrinsically worthwhile in itself, and to bestow worth on everything else.

But most of us later look back on that impression as an illusion, which wears off once we have been with our partners for a while, or have gone through a string of them. There are some people who insist, after every failed love affair, that someday they will meet "the one" who is perfect for them; these people are not unlike those who retain a faith in political utopia. And that faith can, once again, be buttressed with metaphysical arguments of some sort—perhaps human beings have an essence that is fulfilled only when we merge sexually with another person. But such arguments once again represent a failure to find empirical evidence for one's view of the human telos. As with promises of political utopia, here too we have something that on first impression seems a goal that can fulfill our highest aspirations, but that we normally see, on further reflection and with further experience, as having a much more humdrum place in life.

There are also excellent evolutionary explanations for the illusory aura of importance that surrounds erotic love. It makes sense that we should be so taken with erotic love when young, and later regard the claims it seems to make for itself as an illusion. That is how nature leads us first to throw ourselves into bearing children, then to focus instead on raising them. It's not hard to imagine similar reasons why we might at first see radical political programs as of overwhelming importance, but later come to regard that importance as illusory—not hard to imagine that we naturally have a tendency to favor things that will transform our communities when they are under stress, but also a tendency to back off from these transformative visions once the threats recede, and the communities become stable enough to focus, again, on everyday challenges.

So a combination of everyday experience and evolutionary explanation can readily undermine the seeming importance of politics and erotic love. If we bring these sorts of consideration to bear on other candidates for a specific activity that sheds worth on the rest of life, we can quickly make them look hollow as well. When immersed in caring for young children, that can seem an activity of supreme importance, but of all the things we do in life, this one surely comes under the heading of "keeping life going so that we can keep life going." It falls immediately to the *Peanuts* critique: if we are here on earth to raise our children, what are our children here for? Our attachment to child-raising is also easily explicable on biological grounds, and by the fact that any society that wants to survive must reinforce this biological impulse.

How about art? Painting, music, and literature can certainly seem breathtakingly wonderful. But can they be the goal of our whole lives? Perhaps they can if we have an internal essence—a creative "genius"—that requires expression in art. Metaphysical claims like this take us once again too close to the religious faiths we are trying to do without, however, so it would be better to support the importance of art with appeals to experience alone. But our experience of art, joyous as it can be, does not normally lead us to think that it could possibly represent the whole telos of our existence. Could we really work all our lives, struggle to build decent polities, suffer sickness, disaster, and war, just so that everyone can look at paintings or read novels? There is also a question of whether our pleasure in these things really represents an objective value. When we recover from the raptures we experience in the opera house or at the theater, we may worry that our enthusiasm for these things is narcissistic or pretentious, and recall that artistic norms tend to shift in accordance with fashion. Moreover, the appreciation and creation of art is not something that the vast majority of people has ever been able to share, and it seems hard to believe that the overall good for all human beings could be something that only a few achieve.

Then there is the growth of human knowledge. People in academia speak in reverent tones about the growth of knowledge, but rarely have an answer if one asks them *why* knowledge is so important. It's a good question, though. When one strips away the ways in which increased knowledge helps us achieve longer, healthier, and more comfortable lives (promotes the *conditions* for a good life), what is so good about knowledge in itself? On occasion, I've run this question by my fellow academics, who sneer or get angry instead of answering it. But no response could be a surer indication of a dogmatic faith, exactly like the religious faith that these academics abjure. Of course one *could* justify the claim that knowledge is intrinsically important by saying that human beings were designed to seek knowledge, or have a metaphysical essence that is fulfilled in the achievement of knowledge. But to uphold either of these claims would again mean abandoning the attempt to find a secular, naturalistic telos for our lives.

Each of our candidates for a specific sphere of activity that might organize and orient our whole lives has the following three features:

(a) We become attached to the sphere at first by way of strong passion, which raises in us a vision of how this activity could beautify or redeem our whole lives. But the vision comes over time to seem illusory. The pressure of reflection is disturbing to visions produced by passion.

(b) On reflection, we can easily produce a story rooted in evolutionary biology for why we are drawn to this sphere, plus reasons why our societies might encourage these biological impulses. We have learned from Darwin, Marx, Freud, and Foucault to be suspicious of claims to intrinsic value, and readily see them as arising from illusions to which we have a natural tendency, and/or are fostered by social pressures.

(c) Metaphysical theories of one kind or another—often positing an expanded self or soul (a group mind that must be realized in a polis, a shared mind of lovers who complete one another, a creative genius that yearns to be expressed)—could underwrite the importance we attribute to the sphere of activity. But those theories are no better grounded than religious faith, and take us away from the naturalism that we had hoped would underwrite our telos.

These three features do not *disprove* the claims to ultimate value made by advocates of politics, love, art, etc., but they do make those claims more likely to reflect an illusion than to be a true insight into the absolute good. They make it likely, indeed, that the objective value we see in these things is an illusion of exactly the kind that secular people attribute to religious believers.

Let's turn now to our second basket of naturalistic answers to the telic question, on which some general feature of our activities, rather than a specific activity, gives meaning or worth to our lives. This basket subdivides into objectivist and subjectivist components. Objectivists who see value spread across our lives, rather than located in a specific activity, tend to say that participating in a range of activities is itself an absolute good. Subjectivists tend to see the value of human life in whatever we want out of life—in the satisfaction of our preferences. We'll start with the objectivists, then move to the subjectivists.

The troubles we encountered with our first basket of answers to the telic question can readily arise for generalized objectivists as well. Generalized objectivists often urge us to participate in politics and art and the rest of the specific spheres considered above simply because they all seem so valuable. But if it is easy to debunk the considerations leading us to attribute value to each of these spheres, it won't help to aggregate those considerations. If the value we see in *each* sphere of human activity is illusory, then any value we see in *all* the spheres should be just as illusory.

The objectivist may however be relying, not on a value to be found in our experience of these activities, but on a belief that these kinds of activity realize our basic potentials or capacities. Many of the philosophers who uphold a pluralistic view of life's value are Aristotelians, and for Aristotelians, the telos of any living thing consists in realizing its basic potentials or capacities. This is meant to be a naturalistic claim. For Aristotle, the activity of all living things is directed towards a full development of their essence. Human activity is accordingly directed towards the fulfillment of our erotic capacities, political capacities, artistic capacities, etc. But the idea that these capacities belong to our essence—that nature gives us *any* essence—is not credible in the modern day. Aristotelian science, and the account of nature that goes with it, has long been discredited. So it no longer makes sense to draw our picture of the human good from it.

Finally, some people think that it is just common sense that a rich and varied life, realizing many of our potentials, is a good life. And that may *be* common sense, at least in modern-day America. But common sense is untrustworthy when it comes to the telos of our lives, because it is so heavily shaped by social interests and prejudices. That is indeed why secular people, even if they endorse the common-sense belief in realizing our potentials, call on us to resist common-sense views that reflect religious beliefs, or that display sexism or racism. Common sense can get matters of everyday observation wonderfully right—there's no better resource for finding out how to stay cool on a hot summer's day—but on matters remote from everyday observation, it is readily swayed by ideology.

Now the view that we should realize our potentials, and participate in as many of the major spheres of human activity as possible, seems to me the most plausible general view of how life can be objectively valuable. So if its foundations are as weak as I have suggested, it's unlikely that any other objectivist view is likely to do better. Which brings us to subject-ivist approaches to the worth of life. On these approaches, the point of life is whatever we take it to be: we achieve it when we satisfy our desires or preferences. Standardly, although not necessarily, this is taken to be equivalent to an endorsement of seeking pleasure. From ancient times, world views that encourage us to seek pleasure have tended to arise among people who have given up on the hope of finding any objective purpose to life. "Eat, drink, and be merry, for tomorrow we die" is the rallying cry of those who think it foolish or hopeless to find an objective value in what we do.

The problem with this sort of answer to our telic question is that it doesn't adequately respond to the concerns that inspire that question. When I am trying to figure out whether I should go for a high-paying job in advertising or devote myself instead to scientific research, I am asking whether I should *give up* some great pleasures in favor of a good that is nobler, more substantial, etc. than pleasure, and being told that I should do whatever pleases me won't help me. If I am wondering whether to end a difficult or dull marriage or to stick with it for the good of the children, being told that I should do whatever I prefer again does not so much as address my concerns. My question is precisely whether there is some-thing worth living for *aside* from the satisfaction of my preferences, something for the sake of which it might make sense to *sacrifice* some pleasure. So telling me that my subjective satisfactions make life worth living is equivalent to telling me that *nothing* makes life worth living, that life has no point. When I seek a meaning or purpose to life, I am seeking an orienting point by which I can assess pleasure itself, gauge what I *should* prefer: a point, therefore, beyond pleasure and my preferences. I want something to strive for other than pleasure and subjective satis-faction alone, to be able to *take* pleasure, or satisfaction, in something objectively good. I will decide that I might as well live for pleasure alone only if I conclude that there is no objective good. Subjectivist responses to our telic questions are therefore a way of dismissing those questions, not of answering them.

That does not mean that it is impossible to live for pleasure, and some people of course do. Living just for pleasure is often, however, very *un*pleasant. We don't enjoy thinking that we have nothing to live for but enjoyment. Those who structure their lives in a hedonistic way tend to get bored, and find that even experiences that gave great delight for a while lose their excitement after they have been repeated often enough. Notoriously, very rich people are prone to drug and alcohol addiction, or strings of empty love affairs, in a struggle to fight off ennui. In any case, to live for pleasure alone seems childish and shallow. As Aristotle put it long ago, "it would . . . be strange if the [human] end were amusement, and one were to take trouble and suffer hardship all one's life in order to amuse oneself." Pleasure seems unsuited to be the highest goal of beings like us—beings with an ongoing consciousness, which yearns to see the projects in which it engages add up over time. We have a pleasure today; tomorrow it will be gone; and we will take little pleasure in the fact that we had it today. We certainly don't delight in the joys we had years ago. We don't look back on love affairs now long gone and delight in what we felt then, or get comfort from the athletic prowess of our youth as we struggle with failing limbs in old age. On the contrary, we are likely to *envy* our past selves if they had a delightful time years ago, to feel greater pain when reflecting on past pleasures, now beyond our reach, than we would if we had never had them. Pleasure exists in a different time-frame from the one in which we do. It starts and stops, while we continue over time. It has sharp temporal limits, while we are ongoing consciousnesses who yearn to continue eternally and to bring together, in some kind of meaningful whole, all the moments we have experienced, whether pleasurable or painful. As ongoing consciousnesses, and as the subject of all our experiences, not just the pleasurable ones, we are likely to find a truly satisfying highest good only in something that itself builds up over time, and offers more to us—more we can understand, or be aware of—each time we experience it.

That's not to say that anything could be the goal of our lives in which we took *no* pleasure. It makes little sense to say that something that makes us miserable, or bores us, could give our lives worth or meaning. That we enjoy a thing or experience, that we love it, is surely a necessary condition for that thing or experience to be a goal for our lives. But it is not a sufficient condition. The love we feel for art, family, knowledge, etc.—the joy we take in these things—was a major reason we considered them earlier as candidates for the human telos. But it was not enough. Without a fuller story about how these things can give a point to everything we do and suffer, and why people should strive for them even when they do not find them pleasurable, we were unable to make out a case for their ultimate worth; the pleasure we take in them instead seemed like it might *illusorily* present them as objective goods. When we turn our attention to pleasure itself, and press it for the possibility that it could shed value on the whole of our lives, its attractions fade quickly. We see it instead for what I think it is: a subjective condition on value, and a symptom of it, but not, in itself, valuable. This comes out in the paradox that we do not take much pleasure in a life aimed at pleasure. We do not love a life of pleasure.

More generally, it is unlikely that we will love any life whose value is supposed to arise simply from our attitudes toward it. We don't *want* value to be simply projected by us onto the world; we want to find it "out there" instead. This is a serious strike against subjectivist approaches to our ultimate good. It seems eminently reasonable to suppose that one mark of that good, if it exists, is that it enables us to love our lives. This may indeed be part of the definition of our good. But we cannot love a life whose value is supposed to rest just in the fact that we love it. Love can and should be tolerant of a lot of failings, but we do not bestow our love wholly arbitrarily, and we love life, if we do, for *reasons* of some sort, not just because we love it.

One alternative to developing a naturalistic answer to the telic question is to reject the question itself. The psychologist Jonathan Haidt doesn't think much can be said to answer the question, "What is the purpose *of* life?," and suggests we would do better to turn to the question of "purpose *within* life." And he thinks that a combination of "ancient wisdom and modern science" can give us "compelling answers" to that question. We can find all we need, as far as purpose or meaning is concerned, as long as our personalities are in healthy shape, and we have "love, work, and a connection to something larger." If "[you] get the right relationships between yourself and others, between yourself and your work, and between yourself and something larger than yourself, . . . a sense of purpose and meaning will emerge." That's very reassuring. Unfortunately, it isn't true. Tolstoy's devastating *Death of Ivan Ilyich* illustrates well how easily a person who has all these things in place can nevertheless find all "sense of purpose and meaning" fleeing from him when he faces his mortality. Work and love and an engagement in social and cultural activities can all appear, in this context, as *distractions* from the attempt to find purpose and meaning in life, rather than marks of success in that attempt.

Or perhaps I am missing the import of Haidt's appeal to "a connection to something larger"? Many people writing on the value of life use this phrase. But what does it mean? Aren't we *always* connected to something "larger" than ourselves? We fit, spatially, into the world around us—I am connected to Illinois right now, and to the United States, the earth, and the solar system—and we fit, ecologically, into a variety of natural systems. Food and water from a larger world have enabled me to survive ever since I was in the womb, and worms and other creatures from that larger world will make use of my body when I die. This is not a very interesting fact about me, nor does it give me the slightest comfort or sense of purpose and meaning. But what more might I be able to get from my "larger connections"? Or what other larger connections might I aspire to?

Well, I could celebrate the natural universe to which I belong, I suppose. But without religious reasons to *value* the universe, I don't see why I should do that—why it merits celebration. Or I could join a social group of some sort and allow the bonding to something larger I experience there to help me overcome my existential worries. This would not necessarily be a good thing, however—many people have this experience in fanatic religious cults and racist political movements—and there is no obvious reason, even where the group is a decent one, why I should regard the comfort it gives me as a real rather than an illusory indicator of value.

Of course there is a religious interpretation of "connecting to some-thing larger" that does make sense. Secular writers like Haidt are looking precisely for an alternative to religious views of purpose and meaning, however. And in secular terms, "connecting to something larger" seems empty, illusory, or harmful. Without appealing to some such notion, however, Haidt's confidence that we can find "purpose within life" seems overblown. The worry that our ordinary joys and comforts are insuffi-cient reappears, and it is not easy to see how naturalistic considerations can resolve it.

I mentioned Tolstoy a moment ago. Tolstoy reflected on the meaning of life in his *Confession* as well as his *Death of Ivan Ilyich*, demonstrating vividly, there, how empty life seemed to him as long as he remained at a purely secular standpoint. "Why should I live?," he asked—"Why should I wish for anything or do anything? . . . Is there any meaning in my life that will not be destroyed by my inevitably approaching death?" None of the great intellectual achievements of humankind seemed to him to answer this question. Science "does not even acknowledge the question"—it "clearly and precisely answers" questions about all the things *in* our world, but not about what we should live for among them—while philosophy "acknowledges the question but does not answer it." And people aware of this situation, Tolstoy thinks, tend either to throw themselves into sensuous pleasures or feel like committing suicide.

Tolstoy's diagnosis seems to me exactly right, except that I would add distraction and self-delusion as other ways by which people deal with the threat of emptiness. We distract ourselves with drugs or alcohol, with TV and Facebook, with obsessive hobbies or a pursuit of professional status, from the terror that rises up to greet us if we have to think about whether our lives are worthwhile. And when we do stop to do such thinking, we rush to delude ourselves, with the help of banalities that we pick up from inspirational speakers, into supposing that *of course* our lives are worthwhile. What puzzles me is that many contemporary writers, even ones as thoughtful as Haidt, lend strength to these banalities. Tolstoy was more clear-headed.

The arguments I've given against naturalistic candidates for what gives our lives, overall, worth or meaning are hardly decisive. That's fine. I don't think that conclusive proof is possible, as regards telic views. They are too independent of empirical considerations to be susceptible of scientific proof, and too fundamental to ethics to be established by intuitions. So it doesn't bother me if some people respond to the discussion thus far by supposing that they could come up with a good argument for some version of the claims I have dismissed, or for a naturalistic way of understanding worth that I have overlooked. I have tried just to plant a seed of doubt in those who are confident that there are adequate naturalistic answers to our telic questions—to explain why it is not unreasonable to abandon these answers and turn to religious ones instead. In particular, I hope I have given the reader reason to be skeptical of the cheerful complacency with which many contemporary philosophers affirm that *of course* life is worth living, and their support for this affirmation by way of our pre-theoretical intuitions that art, love, political activism, etc. are worthwhile. We do have such intuitions. It is very common for people to pronounce sagely that it is obviously better to see a Shakespeare play rather than a mindless comic movie, to have long-lasting love relationships rather than "friends with benefits," and to work for environmental preservation rather than collecting refrigerator magnets. But why philosophers, who are generally skeptical of common-sense dogmas, should be urging us to trust them on this subject is beyond me. Why should our common-sense intuitions in favor of Shakespeare and do-gooding be any more trustworthy than our common-sense intuitions—shared by at least as many people as those who value Shakespeare over mindless movies—that there must be a God and an afterlife? A belief, even a widespread one, that there is a God doesn't make it so, and a belief that art, love, or politics is worthwhile, even a widespread one, doesn't make that so either. Yet the same philosophers who dismiss religious dogmas are often quick to endorse our dogmas about worth. They don't even seem to mind that the dogmas affirming the value of Shakespeare, etc. are elitist and self-congratulatory—although in general philosophers make it their business to prick elitism and self-congratulation, rather than to go along with them.

If we don't go along with the dogmas, I think we have to admit that it is very difficult to come up with a convincing naturalistic account of the overall human good. That may be in part because of the conception of nature we work with today. Darwinian theories of evolution make our desires, pleasures, and impressions of value all seem like devices for the survival of our genes, and modern physics makes out the universe in general to be a collection of random interactions among material particles. It is hard to see ourselves as having any real value or importance in a world structured like this, or to regard our beliefs *about* value or importance as more than illusions. Still, as noted earlier, the problems with purely naturalistic accounts of value or importance have struck people for centuries, long before the coming of modern views of nature. The shortness of life, the fleetingness of pleasure and its unsuitedness to a consciousness that wants things to add up over time, the fact that our hopes for love and politics tend to be disappointed, the fact that the value we see in things tends to serve the interests of the powerful, or to reflect an unthinking conformism—all these points have been made long ago, and have led many people to wonder whether worth is just an illusion, and we might not be better off giving up on it and living for pleasure alone.

Giving up on the idea is one option, of course, although we have seen that it is not all that pleasant to live for pleasure alone, not easy to do without some conception of ends as truly (objectively) worth striving for. In any case, there is another option. What if the problems we have encountered in making sense of our ultimate or overall good stem from the fact that we have been trying to make clear, naturalistic sense of it? What if our ultimate good is inherently obscure, or obscure when approached in a naturalistic way? Perhaps our good must be obscure if it is to function as it should—to attract our attention, to inspire and guide our activities. Or perhaps there is something about nature, or our nature, that makes it impossible to perceive that good clearly so long as we seek it with naturalistic tools.

Several different points are wrapped up in these suggestions. Let me unpack them a little.

First, by "obscure" I do not mean "unintelligible." If the idea of an ultimate or overall good is unintelligible, it is no better than an illusion, and we ought to give up on it. "Obscure" means *partly* hidden, not wholly so; we might think of a moon behind clouds. The function of the idea of an ultimate good is to orient our lives, to provide something at which our activities can aim. An incoherent telos, or one that we will never understand, cannot function in this way. There could also be no reason to believe that such a thing *is* good—no reason to think that the word "good" suits it. A good that is *difficult* to know, on the other hand, could orient activities for us in part by way of this difficulty. Our difficulties in grasping it give us an incentive always to try to grasp it better. This keeps it attractive to us. A life in which we continually find out somewhat more about what we are trying to accomplish, without ever fully knowing it, would be an interesting life, a life that would be ever-new and that need therefore never bore us. But only an ever-new, ever-interesting life would seem so much as a candidate for a life we could love. And it seems a reasonable criterion of the ultimate good, as we have seen, that it should lead us to love our lives. So a somewhat mysterious end, never fully clear to us even as we understand more about it, might for that reason be a promising candidate for our overall good.

Second, I offered several different reasons for why the good might be obscure or mysterious. It might be obscure inherently—the very notion might be (in part) paradoxical. Or it might be obscure because it is somehow out of nature: fully accessible only in some world other than the one we know. Or, again, it might be obscure because of something about *our* nature: we are too selfish or too wrapped up in material things, perhaps, to grasp it properly.

Each of these possibilities has well known exponents in religious traditions, and many traditions combine several of them. A number of Christian theologians—Tertullian and Kierkegaard, most famously, but also many mystics—have maintained that the notion of divine salvation contains a paradox of some sort; some strands of Buddhism hold a similar view of the enlightenment at which they aim. Many Christians—and Jews, Muslims, and others—have maintained that we will attain our full good only in another life. A different version of this sort of non-naturalism runs through Hindu thought. For Hindus, it is not so much that we will one day inhabit a *different* nature as that *this* nature is illusory, and we can perceive our true good only by piercing through the veil in which it entraps us.

Finally, there is the possibility that our natural tendencies to fear and envy one another, or simply to be attached to our selves, get in the way of perceiving our good clearly. Buddhism, famously, stresses the confusion that comes of attachment to the self, and even if they don't share Buddhist metaphysics, most religious traditions agree that selfishness, greed, and envy cloud our ethical perceptions, and that these tendencies are nonetheless natural to us. For Christians, this is at the heart of original sin; Jews might prefer to talk of the way holiness transcends our given nature. For many religious people, of all these sorts, we will fully transcend our given nature only when we live in another, non-natural world. Others de-emphasize the idea of an afterlife and seek instead for ways in which we might transcend our nature, to some extent at least, in this life.

Each of these possibilities can draw support from the inadequacies in our naturalistic candidates for the good. The idea that the good might contain some sort of paradox fits with the fact that so many things appear strongly to be good to us yet we find reasons, on reflection, to regard that appearance as illusory. The idea that the good might be incompatible with nature fits with the ease with which Darwinian considerations seemed to puncture many of our candidates for goodness, and with the mechanical, purposeless conception of nature with which modern science works. And the idea that *our* nature might be a prime obstacle in the way of our perceiving the good fits with the fact that we both continually seek pleasure and are repelled by the idea of a life aimed only at pleasure. It is also plausible that our daily needs distract us from being able to think clearly about a higher good than survival, and obscure our view of such a good when we do think about it.

But if our highest good is obscure—whether because of something about its nature or because of something about ours—how can we possibly come to grasp it?

Well, suppose we had a text or teaching purporting to describe it that was itself obscure but not incomprehensible, paradoxical but still interpretable. A *poetic* text would fit the bill nicely, since that's how poetry often works, combining obscurity with clarity, puzzling us even as it enlightens us. A poem that purports to come from a supernatural source, or represents a supernatural insight into the natural order, would be even better, since that would give us reason for hoping that it takes us beyond the naturalistic obstacles to perceiving the good properly. And yet better would be a poem that holds out a discipline to us by which we can transform our nature so that we understand our obscure good better, and incorporate what we do understand of it into our daily lives. Of course, the vision of the good in such a text will have to make sense as a reasonable candidate for goodness. It will have to fit in with what else we believe about goodness—our moral beliefs, as well as our intuitions that erotic love, art, knowledge, etc. are good; it will need either to endorse these intuitions or to explain what is wrong with them. It will also need to offer a plausible explanation of why it is so difficult for us to grasp our good overall.

A text that met all these conditions might well be more likely to give us access to that good than our own reason and experience. Which is to say: a *revealed text*, the sort of text that grounds revealed religions, might be our best or only option for gaining access to our highest good. (The good might appear to us only via a "good book.") If attempts to figure out that good on our own—attempts based on our common, naturalistic experience—are doomed to failure, and if the reason for that failure is the obscurity of the highest good, at least when approached in a naturalistic way, then it is not unreasonable to put our trust in a presentation of the good *as* obscure, and *as* supernatural, so long as that presentation fits with our moral beliefs, and gives plausible answers to the problems we encountered when trying to grasp the good naturalistically.

And this I believe is why many otherwise "enlightened" people, committed to modern science and liberal morality, to this day find revealed or sacred texts trustworthy. With the hypothesis of an obscure, non-naturalistic good we come finally to the place where the trust or faith we have been talking about since Chapter 1 has a legitimate role to play. It is not in science or morality but in our search for an adequate telos for our lives that we can make a clear case for trusting an authority over the deliverances of our own reason and experience. It is only as regards this ultimate telos that we have reason to be suspicious of nature, and only in this regard that the idea that what we are looking for might be intrinsically obscure, and that we might therefore need to trust in a guide, makes sense. Revealed texts are guides that open out to us a path to our highest good, and we trust them if and only if we think that there is no more direct way to get there. And that thought, unlike the thought that the Bible or Quran are the last word in scientific or moral theory, is quite a plausible one.

I want to stress that I've laid out just a plausible *hypothesis* (and even then, not in the scientific sense: no empirical evidence can confirm or disconfirm it), not anything remotely like a *proof* that revealed texts can lead us to our highest good. There are a lot of "if"s along the way to an acceptance of this hypothesis, and rational argument alone will never resolve those "if"s. So we will not get a decisive argument for trusting these texts. At best, we can adduce arguments that make such trust appear not *un*reasonable: appear to be a rational faith.

I will say more about rational faith in Chapter 5. First we need to consider in more detail what revealed texts can accomplish.

4

Revelation

In the previous chapter, I offered reasons for supposing that we can find our highest good only by trusting a religious revelation. This revelation must accomplish a number of tasks at once—and must, accordingly, have a complex array of features. Paradigmatically it will be (1) *a poem* that (2) *purports to have a supernatural source* and (3) *presents us with a path by which we can grasp, and realize, a vision of our highest good that is deeply mysterious* but (4) *fits in with what else we believe about goodness* and (5) *offers us a plausible explanation of the errors about our good that come of approaching it naturalistically.*

Let's consider each of these features in some detail.

(1) *A poem*: It is insufficiently noted that the texts grounding practically all revealed or traditional religions are poems. The law of the Torah is embedded in a grand epic poem, and often expressed in highly evocative language (Leviticus 18:16: "Do not stand idly by the blood of your neighbour"). Jesus and the Buddha speak in gnomic parables and epigrams. The Quran and *Tao te Ching* consist entirely of intriguing but enigmatic outpourings. For those who think that revelation should articulate philosophical or moral principles—God should tell us, as clearly as possible, what He wants us to do—the poetic form of revelation can be frustrating. If revelation is instead an attempt to express something intrinsically obscure, then its poetic form makes sense.

Poetry, moreover, intrigues, delights, and awes us. These are the sorts of emotions we need if we are to love our lives, to overcome the ennui we experience when we look at them in a purely naturalistic light. Sometimes the beauty or sublimity of a poem *rests* in its obscurity, in the pleasurable struggle of interpretation to which it gives rise; sometimes poems will just present an ordinary object in a light in which it appears wondrous ("I placed a jar in Tennessee…"). The great poems that found revealed religions do both of these things. They move us in the process by which we interpret them but also help us to see aspects of our everyday lives as wondrous or sublime. They infuse their beauty or sublimity into our world, and thereby enable us to love our lives: a necessary condition, as we have seen, for us to regard them as worthwhile.

It follows that the beauty or sublimity of revealed texts is essential to what they have to teach us religiously. Nor is the religious language we often use about artists—that they are "inspired," that their works are "divine"—as inappropriate as defenders of religion sometimes think. The difference between artistic and prophetic inspiration is not great. What the prophet does—what God does through the prophet—is in large part to beautify our lives. Only a beautiful life can be worthwhile—can be ever-new, ever different from the ordinary or profane: can be holy or redeemed. Of course, beauty is not *enough* for holiness or redemption; art works are not generally, on their own, revelatory. But that just reminds us that a revelatory poem is supposed to illuminate far more than an ordinary artwork does. After all, a revelatory poem presents itself as having an author who comprehends the entire universe. It is a poem *that*, to bring in the second of the characteristics listed at the beginning of this chapter, ...

(2) ... *purports to have a supernatural source* ... If we turn to revelatory texts because we find naturalistic accounts of the worth of life unconvincing, then it is unsurprising that such texts purport to come from a position that stands somehow beyond nature. For theists, especially in the Abrahamic traditions, this means that God spoke the texts, or at least communicated in some way with their authors. For non-theists, the supernatural source of the texts may be an ineffable principle or force underlying the universe—the *tao*, or Brahman—which some especially disciplined or insightful human being managed especially well to capture. Or, as in Buddhism, the text may be seen as having been produced by a person in a condition of enlightenment beyond anything that human beings normally achieve. Even this involves the idea of a position beyond nature as we know it: a "super" natural position.

(3) ... *and presents us with a path by which we can grasp, and realize, a vision of our highest good that is deeply mysterious* ... At the core of revelation, as we have noted before, is the idea that our highest good is essentially mysterious. Consequently, I cannot lay out in a work of philosophy exactly what the highest good unveiled by revelation is supposed to look like. If there is such a thing as revelation, no purely

rational discourse could do that. But at the same time, the highest good of revelation must shape our lives, if it is to *be* our highest good, so it must somehow issue in a mode of action. And in fact every revealed text comes with a path or discipline of some sort, usually combining actions that in some way reflect the mystery of its source ("rituals") with moral practices. Sometimes the text, like the Torah, consists in large part of prescriptions for such a path. Sometimes the path is instead loosely attached to the text: as in the establishment of Easter, or communion, on the basis of moments in the Gospels. But every religion founded in a revealed text comes with a distinctive way of acting—a distinctive way of worshipping, studying, marrying, raising children, mourning the dead, etc. Different religious traditions give different reasons for the paths they lay out. Sometimes the path is supposed to help us achieve holiness or salvation or a release from suffering. Sometimes it can *achieve* nothing and instead expresses our gratitude for having *received* salvation, etc. But in all revealed religions, the path enhances its followers' commitment to its teaching about the highest good, gives them opportunities to understand that teaching better, and enables them to come together in communities where they can guide one another, encourage one another to keep to their shared vision, and spread that vision to others, especially their own children.

In all these ways, the path transforms the goals and desires of the believers, and in most religions that is the main point of keeping to it. The very willingness to humble oneself to a set of actions one has not come up with oneself is transformative and precisely in the way we should expect if our hypothesis about the failure of naturalistic approaches to the highest good is correct. The path leads its followers to restrain or suspend their natural yearnings and expectations, to break out of their self-centeredness and look beyond their own sentiments and modes of reasoning for their goals. Humility is therefore a central virtue in religious traditions, and the paths to which believers humble themselves are supposed to help them better grasp, as well as achieve, a good that, by hypothesis, they could otherwise never see.

(4) ... *but fits in with what else we believe about goodness* ... The good held out by religious revelations must be unknown to us, if there is to be any point to our trusting them, but it cannot be wholly unknown to us if we are to recognize it as good at all. As we have seen, to say that the telos of our lives is obscure cannot be the same as saying that it is

unintelligible. The telic vision of a revealed religion must resonate with what we already believe about goodness. That means, above all, that it must accord with our moral beliefs. People generally turn away from a religious vision if they think that it mandates cruelty or injustice. Nor do most religions—long-established ones, at any rate—in fact offer teachings wildly out of synch with the moralities we come up with on our own. As we saw in Chapter 2, moral beliefs are on the whole independent of telic visions. They are conditions *for* us to pursue telic visions, and to live in communities of people with different such visions. And they tend to be shared across religious traditions—even if those traditions frame morality in different ways. Buddhists and Christians agree that we should give charity, and that we should do so out of concern for the poor, but for the Buddhist, giving charity is also a way of detaching ourselves from our material possessions, while for the Christian, it is also a way of imitating Christ, or expressing gratitude for the undeserved grace we have ourselves received. The telic vision of a revealed religion thus tends to reframe without radically revising our moral beliefs.

But the need for religious visions of the good to resonate with what we believe independently about goodness extends to our telic intuitions as well as our moral ones. In the last chapter, we considered the strong impressions we have that art, knowledge, erotic love, etc. are objectively worthwhile. We concluded that these impressions may be illusory, and that from a Darwinian perspective it is more likely that they are illusory than that they represent insights into an objective good. But if there *is* an objective good, surely it bears some resemblance to what seems to us objectively good: we could hardly recognize it, otherwise, as good at all. Accordingly, a vision of our ultimate good will be more plausible the more it allows that the goodness we see in art, love, knowledge, etc. really is there: that our impression that these things are good is, in general, reliable. Of course, *why* they are good may differ, on these visions, from the explanation we would have been inclined to give without the vision. As with our moral beliefs, a plausible religious vision will tend primarily to reframe rather than to revise our independent telic intuitions about goodness. Art may be good, for a Jew or Christian or Muslim, because it enhances our wonder at the world God has created, or helps increase our awe or love for God; knowledge may help us better understand God; and sex, in the right circumstances, may be a gift from God or a reflection of the unity in difference that is part of God's own being. Different traditions will give different meanings to all these things, different ways of understanding them as means to or constituent parts of our telos. Some traditions may also play down or reject the value we ordinarily place on one or more of these spheres: regarding sex, art, or philosophical speculation as sinful, perhaps. And sometimes these claims will ring true to us, and strengthen our commitment to a particular religious teaching. But if the teaching makes too many claims of this sort, it will undermine its own plausibility. Our telic intuitions provide important clues to what we are seeking in an ultimate good, so if a teaching undermines all of these intuitions, it takes from us the tools by which we can assess it as trustworthy.

(5) . . . *and offers us a plausible explanation of the errors about our good that come of approaching it naturalistically.* As we've seen, the mere fact that revealed religions claim that we cannot fully grasp our ultimate good unless we trust their texts and way of life speaks in favor of the vision they offer us, if we have come to think that naturalistic accounts of that good are bound to fail. As we've also seen, different religious traditions offer different explanations for why naturalistic attempts to find our telos might fail. They may say that the good is intrinsically paradoxical, or that our nature is blocked by sin, or that an excessive attachment to our desires prevents us from seeing the good properly. Or they may say that the material world is an illusion and the true good can only be seen by looking away from it, or through it, to the spiritual reality underneath; or again that there is another world, which we reach only after our bodily deaths, in which alone we can properly perceive the good.

Whether we find these claims convincing will depend on how well we think they explain the various difficulties in naturalistic attempts to locate our telos, and on what metaphysical views, in general—views about the existence and nature of God or the self—strike us as plausible. The metaphysical concerns I set aside in Chapter 1 return here to form part of the basket of criteria by which we assess telic visions. But we also saw in Chapter 1 that there are no knock-down arguments to settle these metaphysical issues. Most of us feel that we can achieve at most a rough sense of what it is reasonable to believe in this area. So we can't, and normally don't, simply base our religious beliefs on metaphysics, but we may use views on these matters to choose among religious claims that otherwise strike us as morally and telically attractive. It's worth noting here that we sometimes face choices within a single religious tradition—between more mystical and more rationalistic versions of

Judaism, say, or more liberal and more conservative ones, or ones with a greater or lesser emphasis on an afterlife—and not just between different traditions. But we are almost never inclined towards one version of our tradition rather than another, or one tradition rather than another, for metaphysical reasons alone. Rather, we balance how plausible we find a religion's view of the good, and of our failure, naturalistically, to perceive or achieve that good, against our metaphysical convictions. We opt for one religion rather than another, or one version of a religion rather than another, always on ethical as well as metaphysical grounds.

I want to stress the role of a text in this account. By "text" I don't necessarily mean something written, just a form of words that is passed along, from one speaker to another, more or less intact; writing is one way of trying to insure that intactness, but an oral poem or code can also count as a text in this sense. (Societies that lack writing, but have, say, bards who pass on certain stories as sacred, can therefore experience revelation.) But we need a particular arrangement of words, and not just general ideas, to disclose a vision of the good human life to us if we are convinced that we cannot discover our overall good on our own, that we need to turn outside ourselves to find it. Texts stand over against our minds, just as physical objects stand over against our eyes and ears; they are independent of and can offer resistance to the internal dialogue we carry out with ourselves. However much we may need, in interpretation, to translate a text into our own terms—and we'll see in Chapter 6 that we need to do that constantly with revealed texts—it never simply dissolves into what we would like it to say. When we seek an idea in a text, we are always aware as we do so that we are engaged with something outside ourselves, different from ourselves, separate from our imaginings and the results of our reasoning. If, then, we are seeking a good that, by hypothesis, we do not think that we can locate by way of our own resources alone, then we should expect to gain access to that good only via a text—a "good book" or other form of words presented to us as sacred. By standing apart from us, by requiring us constantly to wrestle with it rather than to dissolve it into our own beliefs and values, a text preserves the obscurity of the highest good, keeps it out of our full grasp.

In this respect, revealed religion differs sharply from rational religions like Stoicism and Ethical Culture (or many versions of Unitarianism and Reform Judaism), and from the free-floating "spirituality" that has become so popular today. Rational religions maintain *precisely* that we can determine everything there is to know about the good by using our reason alone. Those who say they are "spiritual but not religious," on the other hand, may allow that there is some entity or force in the universe beyond their reason, but think they can achieve whatever relationship they should have with that entity on their own. They resist the idea that they need to turn to a set of words outside of them, passed along by a community and tradition outside of them, to find their highest good—they do not want to be bound by words and teachings that stand outside the internal dialogue they carry on with themselves. This refusal to be bound is why they are not religious. "Religion" in its origin means "to be bound," and religious people usually see themselves as bound: to a tradition, a community, a discipline, and, at the root of all of these things, a text. Within revealed religions, certainly, believers see themselves as bound to a poem with an ethical vision, and that poem is itself passed down in a binding way: by scribes who are obligated to preserve its specific form, sometimes down to quirks of orthography. In so doing, the scribes signal that the teaching they are passing along lies beyond their consciousness, and the consciousness of any of the individuals receiving it. Each believer, instead, must see herself as in dialogue with something that transcends her, goes beyond what is to be found within her own mind. She thereby holds out to herself the hope that she has been addressed by, and is wrestling with, an objective good.

In sum, revelation consists in our encounter with a text, and a reasonable candidate for that text needs:

(a) to be aesthetically inspiring (beautiful, sublime, evocative of love or awe),

(b) to be obscure enough that it meets the need for our highest good to be beyond ready grasp by reason or experience, but accessible enough that we can expect to grasp it better over time,

(c) to offer a path that enables us to structure our lives by it, and transform ourselves so that we can better understand it,

(d) to fit in with what else we believe about the good, and

(e) to offer a believable explanation—including an appeal to plausible metaphysical claims—of why we seem unable to discover our highest good by using our reason and experience alone.

We thus have a variety of criteria by which to assess candidates for revelation.

I don't mean to imply that people generally pick a religion after assessing a variety of them in accordance with these criteria. The process of becoming religious is more like falling in love: dependent on experiences that lead one to feel that a particular tradition addresses one's needs and hopes as nothing else does. Those who become religious— whether in recoil from secular life or in endorsement of the tradition in which they were raised—feel as though a veil of confusion, woven in part of excessive reliance on rational criteria, has lifted from them. But what lies on the other side of the veil is a telic vision, and we recognize it as that on the basis of the ethical criteria I have laid out. These criteria *set the stage* for our experiencing a text as unveiling a telic vision. Compare, again, falling in love. Even if certain experiences draw you to a certain person, you are likely to see yourself, over time, as truly loving that person only if he/she meets certain criteria you have set for yourself, in seeking a romantic partner. Criteria for a good partner play a crucial if inexplicit background role in enabling us to see certain experiences as ones of "falling in love." Similar sorts of criteria make it possible for us to see an experience as revelatory.

Three points to note about all this: First, I have argued for a set of criteria to use when judging whether a particular candidate for revelation is worthy of our trust, but of course not everybody does use such criteria. Many people blindly trust the revealed religion in which they were raised, or that they encountered at a moment of depression or turmoil in their lives. Still, this blind faith is less common than is popularly supposed. Faith is often, not mere conformism, but the result of a choice of some sort. Not only are there thoughtful converts from one religion to another, but many people move from one version of the faith of their parents to another. Others move in or out of religious commitment altogether. And the people making these choices rely at least implicitly on criteria for what sort of religion, if any, makes sense. Those criteria, I suggest, generally run along the lines of the ones I have listed. The criteria are, then, both descriptive and normative: they account for how people *in fact* make choices about religion, as well as prescribing how those choices should be made. That is one reason why I think they are reasonable.

Second, we rely on a *variety* of criteria in assessing candidates for revelation, not a single one. A vision of our highest good that is worthy of our trust has to accomplish a number of different tasks, and it may succeed better in some of these respects than others. Moreover, success in each of these areas is difficult to assess, and balancing the strengths and weaknesses of a religious teaching is accordingly difficult. Consequently, it should not be surprising that different people come to different conclusions about the same candidates for faith, or that the same person may over time change her mind about what is most important in her religion.

Third, it is worth attending to the simple fact *that* we bring a lot to the table in the process by which we put faith in a revelatory vision: that we have choice in this matter, and reasons for our choices. We could not regard a religious teaching as *good*, let alone as the best such teaching, had we no reasons for our commitment to it. Nor indeed could we be truly *committed* to it—rather than merely conditioned, by our upbringing, to follow it.

Now one might suppose that this emphasis on choice is at odds with the emphasis I have placed on trust or faith. How can I talk of commitment to a revelation being a matter of trust or faith if I acknowledge at the same time that it is something we choose? How can I laud the advantages of humbling our modes of reasoning to an authority outside ourselves if underlying that very humbling process is a choice of the relevant authority, a decision that it is more reasonable to trust one authority than others?

There is no real paradox here. On the contrary, choice and trust belong together. On the view I have defended, we *choose to be guided* towards our highest good, when we commit ourselves to a revealed religion. It is just that up to now I have stressed the "guidance" and I am now stressing the "choice." But there is no paradox in choosing to trust a guide. Think of how we follow guides in ordinary life. Even in the simple example I introduced in Chapter 1, Aloysius' advisee has to decide that Aloysius is for some reason worth listening to: that he is wise, likely to have the advisee's best interests at heart, etc. Perhaps that is obvious in the Aloysius case—perhaps Aloysius has a wide reputation for wisdom and decency, or has often helped this particular advisee in the past. Then the element of choice may not come to the fore: the advisee may not see himself as making much of a choice. Elsewhere, there is more difficulty and risk in allowing oneself to be guided, however, and one may be acutely aware of having chosen to enter such a relationship. Once in Fez, a notorious maze of a city where tourist guides have a reputation for getting one lost and then charging extra to lead one home again, I decided to follow a person who offered to help me get back to my hotel. He seemed gentle, straightforward, and uninterested in any reward other than the pleasure of having helped me. And so he proved. But at the moment I decided to follow his lead, I had to assess his apparent qualities very carefully and decide whether they were likely to be misleading or not. Many of us have had such experiences in foreign countries, and most travellers can recount stories that worked out well along with near-disasters. People who allow themselves to be guided in decisions about their diet, career, love life, etc. have similar experiences. In every such case, we have a package of criteria by which to decide whether a potential guide is likely to be trustworthy as well as a sense of whether it is worth trusting anyone, in this respect, rather than trying to handle things by our own lights. But at the end of the day, if we put our trust in a guide, we commit ourselves to a course of action that will in part include steps to which we presume our own reasoning, including the criteria by which we picked our guide, would not have led us. Of course, we may *withdraw* our trust after a while, if our guide comes to seem incompetent or dishonest. As long as we maintain our trust, however, we take some actions based purely on what the guide says, not on our own rational capacities, even if our rational capacities remain present, in the background of the whole relationship.

So trust and reasoning go together in ordinary guidance relationships. They go together in the same way when we put our trust in a revealed religion, as our best hope for grasping and achieving our ultimate good. We do not blindly accept Judaism or Islam or Buddhism, even if we have been raised in it, but assess it against what we know of other religious visions, and against the possibility that we might better realize our highest good, or come to grips with the fact that there is no such thing, by using our rational faculties alone. The criteria informing our choice of a religious guide then remain in place as background conditions for our trust, leading us perhaps to shift the object of that trust a bit (from one synagogue to another, one priest to another). But as long as we maintain the trust, we carry out actions, and uphold doctrines, on which we would not have settled had we not humbled ourselves to the wisdom of another.

Still, our trust is informed by general criteria for trustworthiness; our willingness to follow a guide is itself guided by some idea of where the guidance relationship should lead us. It follows that we will not do just anything that our guide suggests. A religious believer is an *active* follower, not a passive one.

We see this active following, this interaction between trust and reason, in many examples of people who become religious. We also see that people generally come to a religion on the basis of the ethical criteria I have defended—aesthetic, moral, and other concerns that play into our attempt to locate a highest good—rather than metaphysical arguments for the existence of God, or claims for the historical accuracy of the Torah, Gospels, Quran, etc. Consider Eknath Easwaran's account of how he returned to the Hindu tradition in which he had been raised:

[During a midlife crisis in which all the pleasures I had been enjoying began to seem meaningless to me,] . . . I came across a copy of the Upanishads. I had known they existed, of course, but it had never even occurred to me to look into them. My field was Victorian literature; I expected no more relevance from four-thousand-year-old texts than from *Alice in Wonderland*.

"Take the example of the man who has everything," I read with a start of recognition: "young, healthy, strong, good, and cultured, with all the wealth that earth can offer; let us take this as the measure of joy." The comparison was right from my life. "One hundred times that joy is the joy of the gandharvas; but no less joy have those who are illumined."

Gandharvas were pure mythology to me, and what illumination meant I had no idea. But the sublime confidence of this voice, the certitude of something vastly greater than the world offers, poured like sunlight into a long-dark room. . . . I read on. Image after image arrested me: awe-inspiring images, scarcely understood but pregnant with promised meaning, which caught at my heart as a familiar voice tugs at the edge of awareness when you are struggling to wake up.

Or consider a fictional but very realistic account of how a modern Jain, feeling trapped in his conventional roles as husband, father, and heir to a large fortune, returns to the teachings of his ancestral religion:

I sneered [at the monk passing on to me teachings of Mahavira, the founder of Jainism] but at the same time I found myself intrigued by the possibility that this old monk, with his limited knowledge of the world, might know some secret of the heart that could shatter the shell of numbness that enclosed me.

As if reading my mind, the monk said slyly, "What do you lose by hearing Mahavira's description of the skepticism and nihilism that disturb a man when he finds he is not free, although he continues to perform the role that society requires of him?"

I was taken aback. "Mahavira spoke about these things?"

The monk was amused by my reaction and offered to instruct me further.

Over the months the monk's teachings continued to surprise me. He was able to predict how I would feel long before I arrived at the emotion myself, describing to me the states of my despair with greater accuracy than I seemed able to experience them.

In both these cases, a religious tradition grabs the attention of the potential believer because it seems to have powerful insights into the ultimate human good, and why that good is so elusive, because it expresses these insights in "arresting," "awe-inspiring," and psychologically astute ways, and because it addresses "the heart" as well as the intellect, breaking through "darkness" and "numbness." And in both cases, the believer takes time to enter the tradition more fully, treating the initial moment of attraction to it as a spur to further study, guided by the hope of further illumination into the goodness he has glimpsed. Trust in a book, or a monk explicating a book, is instigated and conditioned for both of these people by the hope that it will lead in a particular direction. It is never—not in the beginning, and not as they proceed along their religious path—blind or unthinking.

For my own part, I chose to take the Torah as my telic authority—I was raised in a Jewish home, but became more observant in my late teens—above all because I found in it a sublime presentation of the evils of idolatry, and a plausible solution to those evils. The idea that idolatry is the great source of both moral evil and telic blindness was immensely compelling to me, and I saw the Torah as both teaching that in its narratives and offering a comprehensive discipline to wean us from idolatry. I understood idolatry fundamentally to be worshipping ourselves (worshipping "the works of our own hands," in the Bible's language): projecting objects of our desires before us as if they were gods—unquestionable, absolute goods—and sacrificing everything else in their pursuit. And this self-worship seemed to me the main source of oppression and callousness, as well as, for the self-worshipper him or herself, a desperate ennui. In the Torah, the self-worship of a powerful Pharaoh underwrites a brutal system of slavery, and prevents him from being able to back away from his own oppressive tendencies. Later, the inclination to idolatry of the newly-freed slaves leads them to a blind worship of gold and of sex (Exodus 32, Numbers 25): of the objects of their own desires rather than an absolute, spiritual good that transcends and can challenge those desires. This portrayal of evil, and of human psychology, rang true to me. From what I had read and experienced, I found it easy to believe that oppressive social systems are upheld by just such selfishness and arrogance, and that that same self-centeredness blocks us, individually, from appreciating goods that lie beyond our desires.

It made eminent sense to me, then, that God's true revelation—the revelation, at least, that made best sense for *me* to trust—would take the form of a story in which the true good can be seen only when one comes out from under spiritual and physical slavery, and takes on an uncompromising commitment to break oneself of idolatry. And it made sense to me that that commitment could be fostered only by a law that requires us both to protect the weaker members of society (the poor, the widow and orphan, the stranger) and to check our selfish desires. The law of the Torah winds its way through every corner of our lives in order to remind us, and help us, not to idolize food, sex, clothing, money, or any other object of our desires. It keeps us from closing in on ourselves, from resting complacently with the ends that our biology and socialization have instilled in us, and urges us instead to open our pursuits of these goods to the guidance of an absolute Good that transcends them: that can, therefore, harmonize them with the pursuits of our fellow human beings, and restrain them sufficiently that we might glimpse a kind of goodness, mysterious and ever-new, beyond anything we have conceived. The Torah calls such restraint "holiness," and teaches that only in a state of holiness can we come into the presence of God.

I continue to find this conception of what the pursuit of our highest good might look like, and the stories by which it was conveyed, both plausible and moving. They are the aspects of the Torah that reassure me whenever I have doubts about it: that give me some confidence that *if* there is a God, and God has revealed the highest good to human beings, the Torah is the best candidate I have found for that revelation. Breaking through all idols and walking humbly before a God Who transcends everything familiar to us strikes me as the best candidate for what we need to do if we are to perceive and achieve our highest good. And insofar as I am drawn by this vision of the good, I see myself as standing, each day, at Sinai: in a space of revelation.

I want to stress the role of aesthetic as well as moral considerations in this assessment of the Torah. Aesthetic virtues, as we saw earlier, are an important mark of the telic; we seek a highest good that is simultaneously moral and beautiful. So the Jewish tradition's struggle against idolatry, if it is to be a reasonable way of pursuing our highest good, ought to be beautiful as well as moral. Indeed, its aesthetic aspects ought to be interwoven with its moral virtues. Religious Jews who marched for civil rights in Selma—Abraham Joshua Heschel called this "praying with his feet"—or who, today, try to protect Palestinian orchards from destruction by Jewish settlers (there is no idolatry more dangerous than the idolatry in our own homes, and the greatest moral danger Jews face today is an idolatry of land, at the expense of other people's humanity) see the cause they support as not just morally right but a way of pulling themselves out of the pride and self-centeredness that block their ability to perceive our highest good. On the other hand, keeping the Sabbath, with its many intrinsic beauties and the opportunities it offers for stopping to wonder at the beauty of our world, is not just affectively powerful but something that teaches humility, the value of community, and other moral qualities. Jewish law beautifies morality and moralizes beauty, which fits wonderfully with what, as I understand it, our highest good, or path to such a good, ought to achieve.

I also want to stress the fact that I came to the Torah—as the Hindu and Jain characters in my earlier examples came to their religions— primarily by way of ethical considerations, not metaphysical or historical arguments. Whether there ever was an historical Abraham or Moses, and whether Jews were ever enslaved in Egypt and miraculously released from bondage, does not matter much to the way in which the Torah and its law, on my view, convey a vision of and path to the highest good. Whether there is a God matters much more, but all I need, in order to regard the telic vision of the Torah as worthy of my trust, is the absence of a *disproof* of God's existence. I need not have a proof of God, and indeed am more inclined to take the supreme wisdom I see in the Torah as one reason *for* belief in God than to base my respect for the Torah on prior arguments for God's existence. I also hope that pursuing the path laid out for me by the Torah may help me find further reasons to believe in God, and a better understanding of what God might be like.

Two further points: First, what brought me to the Torah, and the Hindu and Jain in my earlier examples to their sacred texts, was the *general* vision we found in our texts, not a sense of awe or illumination in response to every verse. Part of what I believe, when I put my faith in the Torah, is that it is possible to read each of its verses to support the vision that I see in the whole, but that vision is read out of the whole, not from each sentence on its own. It's hard to imagine what it would mean to find every sentence of a text revelatory; that's not how we find wisdom in any sort of discourse, and seems particularly ill-suited to a vision that is supposed to meet the complex criteria that we need to assess a revelation. In any case, religious people are in fact always moved to their faith, not by an individual verse here or there, but by a general view they find in their texts, or by certain striking parables, doctrines, or moments in the life of their religious teachers. They then use this view or these striking moments to interpret the rest of their sacred texts. This allows for reinterpretation of particular verses in terms of the core vision—an extremely important practice, as we shall see in Chapter 6.

Second, the fact that my examples all concern people turning to more stringent or intense versions of the religion of their families does not, I think, vitiate the claim that their religiousness depends to a significant degree on choice, on rational assessment among alternatives. I was raised as a Jew—indeed in a family that cared a good deal about the Jewish tradition. Easwaran, and the Jain in the novel I quoted from, also returned to the tradition of their ancestors rather than adopting a new religion. One might take these cases to be evidence that my talk about assessing religious traditions for their merits is hollow: one might say that most people who become religious just conform to a tradition in which they have been socialized. I don't think this can be right, however, in part because religious people often wind up taking on practices and beliefs wholly unlike anything their family and friends urged on them in childhood. That is certainly true in my own case, and seems, from his description, to be true of Easwaran as well. And if we allow for the possibility that there could be a variety of revelations of the highest good, each suited to some people and not to others, then it doesn't seem to me problematic that the revelation to which a particular person turns might normally be some version of the one his or her family embraced (more on this possibility in Chapter 7). Certainly, that is how the Jewish tradition understands the process of becoming religious. The

Torah calls over and over on parents to teach its stories and law to their children, and bring their children into the observance of the Sabbath and holidays. Hindu and Confucian traditions have a similar conception of themselves, as do many small tribal religions. Christianity and Buddhism, by contrast, have a more individualist tendency, urging their followers to come to them one by one, rather than as members of a family. Presumably, the fact that a tradition sees religious commitment as best passed down in families will help support its claims for those who share my intuitions about the way such commitments work, while those with more individualist intuitions will be drawn to more individualist religions. This is itself one of the ways in which the basket of criteria by which we select a religion is varied enough to lead different people to different religions.

I've thus far discussed coming to a revelation as if it occurred at a single moment, in which one realizes that one's secular past has been shallow or misguided and sees a religious path as leading to a better conception of the human telos. But one may also shift one's conception of that telos, and how the religion should guide one towards it, as one moves along the path. That is one *purpose* of the path.

In my own case, as I've learned more about Judaism and pursued its ritual path more fully, I've found many things appealing about it in addition to what originally attracted me to it: the openness of Jewish learning to self-criticism and disagreement, for instance, or the rich creativity of Jewish methods of interpretation, or the sensitivity with which Jewish law adapts to the needs of its communities. I've also found some features of Jews and Judaism *un*attractive. Some of our ritual practices seem mechanical or silly. Some rabbis I've encountered make implausible metaphysical claims or ground Judaism in spurious science and history. Much worse are moral problems with the contemporary Jewish community. The increasing racism in Israel, especially among Orthodox Jews, and the use of legal fictions to justify oppressing and humiliating Palestinians, at times leads me to wonder whether I should give up on Judaism altogether. I have similar feelings when confronted with the racism and dishonesty of some religious Jews in the United States. Surely God could not be the source of a vision of goodness that has these appalling attitudes and practices as its upshot. But then I think of the many Jewish human rights groups that resist these evils—sometimes run by

Orthodox Jews—and of the fact that the Torah, and its traditional interpretations, include many admonitions that can be used against racism and injustice. I also remind myself that the moral problems of the Jewish community have parallels in every other community, and that the existence of strongly self-critical voices within it, like the Jewish human rights groups, is by contrast rather unusual. These thoughts keep me within my tradition, restore my sense that the Jewish telic vision really does represent my best shot at realizing my highest good—the route that is most likely to give me, if not necessarily everyone, access to that good.

Similarly, the problems I have with some Jewish ritual practices, and the teachings of some of our religious leaders, are almost always shared by other Jews. With their help, I've found ways of enlivening rituals, and replacing shallow or silly teachings with plausible and deep ones. Any temptation I have to abandon the Jewish path has thus far been overcome by such means. Which is to say that I am kept on that path by a *community* that works together in trying to interpret the Torah so that it yields a moral as well as beautiful life. It is also to say that religious trust or faith is not an all-or-nothing affair, embraced at one moment and then fixed forever, but an ongoing process that responds to the various demands that life puts on us; it resembles a marriage rather than a wedding. The ongoing decision of believers to stick with a particular path has to be made and re-made over time. It depends on our continuing to find that path beautiful, morally appropriate, and plausible—or at least *more* beautiful, morally appropriate, and plausible than the alternatives. And we are aided in this ongoing decision by a community with which we share our path, and the modes of interpretation it develops to keep the path decent and inspiring.

We'll see in more detail how communities, and their shared modes of interpretation, shape religious commitments in Chapter 6. First we need to examine more closely the trust or faith I have been talking about.

5

Ethical Faith

Some religious believers will complain about what I have said thus far:

My faith is not just in a *book*. My faith is in *God* (or in Brahman, the *tao*, etc.) and the salvation (enlightenment, reconciliation) He holds out to me. I believe that I will live after death and have my sins forgiven, or unite with a cosmic spirit, or grasp the nothingness of my self and thereby end my suffering. These are factual claims, and if they are not true, my faith is in vain. Telling me just that my sacred scriptures are a trustworthy guide to finding life valuable does me no good. How does *that* help show that my beliefs about God and an afterlife (etc.) are true?

Well, I myself believe in a God and an afterlife, and find it hard to see how our earthly lives can be worthwhile if these beliefs are false. So when I say that I trust the Torah to lead me to my highest good, I mean among other things that I trust it to give me greater confidence in God's existence, and in the existence of an afterlife. But my reasons for believing in a God and an afterlife are much like my reasons for believing in the Torah: I take the ethical value of believing these things to be reasons to think that they are true.

How can that be? How can ethical considerations ever serve as reasons to believe a factual claim?

I want here to bring in an important idea of Immanuel Kant's: that it can be reasonable to hold what he calls a "moral faith" in the existence of certain metaphysical entities, like God and an afterlife, even if we cannot provide any empirical evidence or a priori argument for them. Kant maintains that our highest good consists in an eternal life that combines moral action with happiness, and that moral action seems pointless unless this good is attainable. He also acknowledges that eternal life is unattainable unless there is a God. But he does not think that there is empirical evidence, or adequate a priori argument, to show that there is a God or an afterlife. That does not matter, he says: the fact that these are presuppositions for the existence of the highest good is reason enough to believe in them. After all, neither empirical evidence nor a priori argument rules *out* the existence of God and an afterlife. So it is not *un*reasonable to believe in these things. And the fact that they make sense of our moral activity gives us positive reason *to* believe in them. They are objects of a reasonable hope, Kant says, and a person committed to morality will maintain such a hope in order to make sense of her actions. She could not reasonably act otherwise.

Not every link in this chain of argument is fully convincing, and in any case I do not agree with Kant that our highest good consists in a simple combination of morality with happiness. As I have argued in previous chapters, I regard our highest good as instead essentially obscure to us: its very nature requires revelation. I also see our highest good as necessary for us to make sense of our activity as a whole, not just our moral activity. I prefer therefore to speak of an "ethical" rather than a "moral" faith, in accordance with the distinction between "ethics" and "morality" introduced in Chapter 2. But with these caveats, I want to defend Kant's proposal that we can reasonably believe in certain factual claims if they cannot be disproven by science or logic, and are necessary to our ability to see our lives as worthwhile.

What does it mean to believe in a factual claim, while acknowledging that one has no evidence or direct argument for it? For Kant, it means that we see ourselves as having to regard it as true in the course of our actions. He proposes a practical faith—a faith manifested in our practice and necessary to it. Now, there are many cases in everyday life in which we take things to be true as a presupposition of our practice, even though we do not have adequate evidence for them. Consider a district attorney (DA) dealing with a murder or rape case in which one plausible suspect is a member of a despised minority. If the evidence overwhelmingly points to this suspect, the DA would be derelict in her duty if she did not arrest that suspect. But if the evidence is more mixed—there are other plausible suspects—and the DA has good reason to fear that charging this suspect will inflame local prejudices, then it is perfectly reasonable for her first to do everything she can to investigate the other suspects. As she does so, she may say that she "takes it as her working hypothesis" that one of the other suspects is guilty. This "taking something as a working hypothesis" is a practical belief, which rests on moral principles as much as evidence.

Or imagine a husband who has some evidence, but not overwhelming evidence, that his wife is having an affair. Some husbands will react to such evidence by immediately interrogating their wives, or checking into everything their wives have done lately. Sometimes they are right to do this—they may end a long-dysfunctional relationship—but in many cases they will unnecessarily destroy the trust in their marriage, and make a loving and loyal spouse miserable. A reasonable person will weigh evidence here, and proceed suspiciously if the evidence is strong. But if it is not strong, many reasonable people will decide to believe that their wives are faithful. We may say that they "take the faithfulness of their wives as a working hypothesis"; but a more natural way to put it is simply that they *trust* their wives, and hope that that trust is merited. This trust is a good example of a moral faith: a faith in certain factual claims that is underwritten by moral reasons as much as by empirical evidence.

Now, the words "faith" or "trust" fit the second of these cases better than the first. "Taking something as a working hypothesis" sounds quite different from "trusting" or "hoping" that that something is true; there is a warmth in the latter case that is missing from the former. But there will normally be some hope involved in the decision of a DA to pursue suspects other than the one that her neighbors would like to lynch, and there is a certain amount of "adopting a working hypothesis" in the decision of a husband who puts his suspicions out of mind and trusts his wife. The cooler and warmer versions of this practical attitude belong on a spectrum, and most instances involve a bit of both. That is certainly the case with the religious instances that concern us here. I both take the existence of God and an afterlife as my working hypothesis, and hope that there is a God and an afterlife. Sometimes it feels more like I am doing the former; sometimes I am intensely aware of the element of hope.

In either case, of course, a skeptic might suggest that I am indulging in wishful thinking. Kant's moral faith has been described as a kind of wishful thinking ever since he first introduced the idea. May I not equally well believe that the ideally beautiful woman of my fantasies must exist, Thomas Wizenmann asked Kant? Wizenmann was himself a devout Christian, but he thought Kant's argument for belief in God was silly: it would allow one to posit the existence of anything one wanted to believe in, so long as one supposed that the existence of that thing was somehow necessary to one's actions. One hears the same sorts of complaint today. Why stop at God and an afterlife, ask Kant's critics? Why not also posit the existence of the Easter bunny? Surely it too might help make our lives worthwhile.

To which Kant had several answers. First, we are *forced* to take a stand on factual claims that affect our activity as a whole, but we are not forced to take such a stand on claims that affect some particular, limited project, like the search for an erotic partner that Wizenmann describes. And second, our activity as a whole includes what we do to figure out what is real and what is unreal—the very activity that, in the form of science, may rule out the existence of God, afterlives, etc. So if it undermines the presuppositions of all our activity, science may undermine the reasons why we engage in *it*. A third argument probably lurks in the background of these claims: that science cannot rule out the existence of a being beyond all of nature—as God, properly conceived, must be—while it can rule out the existence of beings which, if they existed, would have to have a place *within* nature, like the Easter bunny. So positing the existence of God—a properly-conceived God, at least, not a glorified superhero like Zeus or the "old man in the sky" of much popular religion—does not run into the difficulties that Wizenmann and his heirs attribute to it.

Let me elaborate these points a little.

In what sense is a stance on the existence of God (or Brahman or the *tao* or other elements of a religious metaphysics) "forced" from us? We do not *feel* forced to take such a stance, and many people in fact regard themselves as agnostics: abstaining from a stance either for or against God's existence. But we *are* forced to take a stance on what makes life worth living. As noted in Chapter 3, we inevitably take such a stance in the way we organize our lives, whatever we may think we are doing. Even the person who says "nothing really matters; one can do whatever one likes with one's life," thereby takes up a view of ultimate worth. And this view depends on a variety of metaphysical beliefs: that there is *no* God, for instance, no being who has established an ideal for us to strive towards, or can show us a good beyond what we seek naturally. The same goes for other views of worth. We saw in Chapter 3 that we use metaphysical claims of one sort or another to underwrite beliefs that life is made worthwhile by eros, art, politics, and the like. Willy-nilly we take a stance on metaphysical issues—factual matters that transcend what we can establish empirically—whenever we pursue one or another conception of our ultimate good, or allow such an idea to guide our actions. Kant thinks that the only conception of our ultimate good that makes sense, when we think it through, is one that presupposes the existence of God. In that sense, then, he takes belief in God to be rationally necessary: a belief that we need in order to make sense of our practice is one that reason demands of us, regardless of whether we have evidence for it. And without quite going along with Kant's claim that belief in *God*, specifically, is necessary for our actions, I think that he is right to regard metaphysical claims as reasonable whenever they are practically necessary. A reasonable person must make sense of what she is trying to do with her life, before worrying about what science tells her.

We can make a yet stronger point. One of the things that belongs among our actions, after all—that is indeed crucial to everything we try to do—is a decision concerning what conception of reality to adopt. We are not forced to accept experience as real, nor yet to regard science as the best explanation of experience. Many people, in many places and times, have not used anything like science as their touchstone of reality, and even now some try to find out about the world by turning to astrologers or cult leaders rather than to scientists. The willingness to heed what scientists tell us itself belongs among our decisions, and affects most of our other decisions. It helps determine what medicines we take, what food we eat, and what technology we use. It determines whether we turn to astrologers, etc. for guidance about our marriages or careers. But when we use or refuse to use science in any of these ways, we are always making a choice. Nothing about the workings of science, including its empirical success, can force us to regard it as reliable. We make a choice even if we accept prior empirical success as a guide to future empirical success. And we make a further choice if we regard empirical evidence as telling us all we need to know about reality. Empirical evidence alone cannot prove that all real objects are empirical ones; that would be circular. Instead we must *decide, choose*, to regard experience as our only guide to reality, and that choice, like all other choices, is reasonable only if guided by the principles of practical reason. So we choose the degree to which we rely on empirical evidence, or the scientific theories based on such evidence, in the light of what we mean to do with our lives: in the light of what we take to be our highest good. Consequently, any presuppositions we make in the course of setting or selecting a conception of our highest good must lie behind our very decision to accept science itself (to whatever extent we do accept it).

Which means that science itself cannot alone establish whether any objects presupposed by our conception of the highest good are real. We must instead presuppose their reality in the process of deciding whether or not to endorse science. In a remarkable section of the *Republic*, Plato suggested that the good is prior to reality and truth: we determine what is real and true only in the light of the good. I wouldn't go quite as far as that—surely we also endorse a conception of goodness only in the light of our conception of reality and truth. But there is at least a chicken-and-egg problem here: we make choices about what conceptions of reality to accept in the light of what we consider good as well as the other way around. That is enough for ethical commitments to infect our metaphysics. If we are concerned simply about what we experience during our lifetimes, we may want to accept a purely scientific conception of reality; if we think that there may be a non-experiential reality, and/or some sort of experience after our deaths, then we may plunk for a metaphysics in which scientists do not have the last word about what counts as real. In any case, *everyone*, not just religious people, needs to make a decision about what to count as reality, and that means that the decision of religious people to keep open, if only as a working hypothesis or matter of hope, the possibility that there might be a God and an afterlife is no more a rejection of what the outside world tells us than the secular person's decision to assume that there cannot be any such thing. We all have to decide what to count as real as part of our attempt to make overall sense of our lives.

To assume that there is a God is therefore no more arbitrary than to assume that there is no God, or that all of reality is scientifically investigable. All of us need to combine metaphysical and ethical views when it comes to the fundamental principles guiding our lives, and the important thing is simply to find a combination that makes sense as a whole. We must take a holistic view of reality and goodness, adjusting our ethical views in response to experience or scientific theory and adjusting our conception of reality in response to ethical pressure. Our views need to fit together as a whole, to make plausible ethical as well as scientific and metaphysical sense. That rules out beliefs in the Easter bunny. All scientific evidence tells against its existence; it is metaphysically construed such that it should be scientifically ascertainable if it does exist;

and its existence is surely unnecessary to any plausible view of our highest good. A God Whose existence cannot be proven or disproven by science, because He/She/It underlies the entire empirical world that science studies, and in Whom we need to believe in order to make sense of our highest good, is not a similarly arbitrary object of belief. These considerations make reasonable a trust or hope that there is such a God. And similar considerations can make reasonable a trust in the existence of the *tao* or Brahman, or the attainability of Buddhist enlightenment.

In sum, trust in a revealed text normally entails trust in the existence of certain metaphysical beings or principles, but trusting that these things exist need not be mere wishful thinking. Rather, such trust is or can be a reasonable presupposition of our ethical activity, just as the belief that secular people maintain in the non-existence of metaphysical entities may be a reasonable presupposition of their ethical practice. At the same time, maintaining a reasonable faith or trust in these entities is emphatically not the same as having a proof that they exist. We can have proof only within certain tightly circumscribed modes of cognition—science and mathematics, paradigmatically—and here we are talking about principles on the basis of which we decide whether and how to use these modes of cognition at all. When we make our fundamental telic decisions, we are beyond our ordinary language-games for counting things as "real" or "unreal." In this murky and indeterminate meta-cognitive space we must feel our way toward reasonable belief patchily, putting together a piece of our world-picture here together with another bit there in a way that relies on judgment—a "seat of the pants" sense of what is reasonable—rather than a clear decision-procedure. The foundations of our way of life, which include our conception of reality and of how to investigate reality, are holistic rather than dependent on any single principle, and infused throughout by what we care about, not dictated by a value-free grasp of truth.

But now one might worry that I have gone too far in the opposite direction, from the faith in a text I defended in previous chapters to a faith just in metaphysical entities like God or the *tao*, not in a text at all. I am supposed to be giving a defense of faith in *revealed* religion, to which authoritative texts are central, but it might now seem that revelation is superfluous. If we have practical reason to believe in certain metaphysical entities, our faith should be directly in them, not in a text or teaching that merely presupposes them.

The point, of course, is that the metaphysical entities and the revealed text go together, if I am right about the essential obscurity of our highest good. Metaphysical claims about God or the *tao* or self-less enlightenment belong to the holistic package guiding our trust in a particular revealed vision, but the vision transcends those claims, and informs and sharpens our understanding of them. Metaphysical claims that we come to by reason will not alone yield up a highest good that, by hypothesis, our nature—our reason and empirical faculties—is unable to grasp. We must instead hope or trust that we will be able to grasp such a good by following the lead of a revealed text or teaching. At the same time, our hope or trust in the vision presented by such a teaching makes sense only if that vision is beautiful, morally admirable, and metaphysically plausible. So we use metaphysical principles in the course of assessing candidates for revelation, but those principles provide just a *scaffolding* for the vision we trust, not its content.

More concretely, a person who comes to believe in God on the basis of philosophical arguments—whether those sketched here or any others—is unlikely to learn much from these arguments about what *sort* of God she believes in. Is this a God who redeems us from sin or frees us from mental slavery? A God who primarily loves us or a God who primarily metes out justice? A God wholly accessible to reason or a God whom we must encounter in mystical trances? Most likely, it is just the bare idea of a perfect Being, who serves as the purpose of the universe or is in some other way its source. This abstract and vague God is pretty much all that philosophical argument can yield, and it is hardly a God who will give us a point for living, an orienting goal for our lives, like the God of Judaism or Islam. *Revelation* gives us that sort of God, and *only* revelation can do that—although our very belief that a particular text is revealed will depend on our prior moral, telic, and metaphysical intuitions. Revelation promises us that we can be led from the thin, abstract conception of God we might come up with by philosophical means to a fuller, richer God who can orient our lives, and enable us to see them as worthwhile. If our willingness to trust a revealed text to lead us to such a place is conditioned in part by metaphysical beliefs, those beliefs are also enriched and sharpened by the revelation in which we trust. I am much more willing to believe in the God of the Hebrew

Scriptures, as I understand them—stern but compassionate, insisting that we treat our fellow human beings decently but also inviting us into His presence—than in the God posited by philosophers, even though one reason I trust the Hebrew Scriptures is that I think they mesh fairly well (when interpreted in certain ways) with plausible philosophical accounts of God. So there is a degree of circularity in my belief. But it is not a vicious circularity. Our telic beliefs are holistic, defined and strengthened by a network of connections with one another. Neither faith in a revealed vision nor the philosophical reasoning by which we interpret such visions can stand alone: they must be interwoven with one another.

I would add that I have never met anyone who was religious on the basis of philosophical reasoning alone. We turn to religion because we seek a vision of the highest good that we can love, and that enables us to love our lives. But we do not, cannot, love reason alone, or anything at which we arrive by reason alone. What inspires love in us is not reason but something else. So if we are to love our lives, something other than argument will have to orient them. This is what we find in our obscure and poetic religious visions. Their very obscurity is tantalizing, their poetry inspiring, and they give us joy, in part, by the struggle in which we have to engage to understand them better. In any case, religious visions must *move* us, not merely seem plausible to us. Only then will we have any reason to seek metaphysical principles by which to interpret them. So without our revealed texts and teachings, we would have no telic faith; philosophical argument provides at most necessary conditions for an appropriate object of that faith, and a clarification of what faith entails. Philosophy provides revelation with a context in which its splendor—its enigmatically inspiring vision of our good— can shine. Metaphysical arguments, moral principles, telic intuitions, and a trusting submission to a revealed text may all fit together in a holistic structure, but trust in the text is the jewel in that crown. Without that, the rest will not constitute a religious faith. We will not humble our faculties to a good beyond their full grasp, and may as well go back to the attempt to figure out our highest good using reason alone.

So faith and reason go together: reason conditions faith and faith complements reason. Augustine taught this combination long ago, and ibn Rushd, Maimonides, and Aquinas did so as well. Nor should the point be terribly surprising. As we saw in the previous chapter, whenever we so much as trust a guide to show us around a city, our trust is conditioned by rational conditions, but those conditions do not get us where we want to go by themselves. People talk a lot of nonsense today about trust or faith being antithetical to reason. There is of course such a thing as a blind or irrational faith. But faith does not have to be blind, and serious religious believers try to make sure that it is not.

6

Receiving Revelation

By hypothesis, the good presented to us by our revealed texts is obscure. By hypothesis also, however, it cannot be wholly obscure, else we could not recognize it as good at all, and it could not shape or orient our lives. So our independent understanding of goodness must play a role in our relationship to revelation. For all the trusting submission a revealed teaching may demand of us, we must remain autonomous in that submission. I have already noted that moral principles, telic intuitions, and metaphysical arguments help us define certain encounters with a text as experiences of revelation. Now we need to examine how these independent, rational glimpses of the good affect the way we receive revealed texts over time—interpret them, incorporate them into our activities, and build communities together with similarly-minded interpreters and agents.

That human autonomy plays an essential role in the reception of revelation is widely recognized by revealed religions themselves. Moses urges the Israelites to "choose life" (Deuteronomy 30:19)—choose the path of the Torah. The implication is that they have other options. The Jewish tradition has in addition two contrasting legends, which together express beautifully the fact that revealed teachings must be both beyond our autonomy and dependent on it. According to one legend, God held Mount Sinai over the Israelites' heads and threatened to bury them beneath it if they didn't accept the Torah. According to the other, God asked all the peoples of the earth if they would accept the Torah and the Israelites received it because only they said yes. The two legends together capture the paradox that a revealed teaching must call for submission but can become ours only if we accept it freely. In Judaism the emphasis is indeed on the free acceptance, since the legend about the mountain being held over people's heads is followed immediately by a rabbinic complaint that such a threat would constitute a charge against the covenant between God and the Israelites—no contract can depend on a threat. The rabbinic process of receiving the Torah is also marked throughout by autonomous reasoning.

In the Gospels, the idea that Christ's love must be accepted freely comes out in a much-quoted dialogue between Jesus and Martha. Jesus says, "I am the resurrection and the life; he who believes in me . . . shall never die." He then asks Martha, "Do you believe this?" and she replies, "Yes, Lord." (John 11:25–27). He also asks Simon Peter three times, in the last chapter of John, "Do you love me?", and charges him with care of his "sheep" only after Peter responds, each time, that he does. These conversations encapsulate Jesus' relationship with his followers, and despite the many forced conversions carried out by Christians, and other uses of violence and brutality to subdue the world in the name of Christ, mainstream Christian churches have always held that faith cannot be compelled.

The Quran, like the Torah, presents itself as offering humanity a choice between "two highways" (90:10), and like Christianity proclaims that there should be "no compulsion in matters of faith" (2:256). In practice, Muslims, like Christians, have not infrequently failed to live up to this ideal of free faith, but mainstream Islam has always upheld it as the ideal mode of religious commitment.

The idea in each of these traditions—and Eastern religions, especially Buddhism, place an even greater emphasis on individual assent to their teachings—is that revelation is not truly revelation at all unless it is received as such by the people to whom it is addressed. God cannot speak to me if I do not listen, cannot give me something if I refuse to take it. The reception of revealed teaching is therefore integral to the very process of revelation itself. If we want to heed God's word, we need to understand it, to put it in terms that make sense to us and that we can employ to shape our lives. It does not follow that God's word consists in whatever we make of it, as progressive religious believers sometimes suggest. Interpreting what a speaker says is not the same as making him say what we would like to hear. But communication takes place only where the listener tries actively to make sense of what she hears; even God's communication to us requires our participation.

All this needs to be said because on some popular religious views, revealed teachings are self-explanatory, and should be followed literally rather than by way of elaborate interpretation. Otherwise—say the so-called "fundamentalists" who promote such a model—we will impose our human views on God's word. We should instead be completely passive in relation to that word, taking it in as if it were transparent, rather than trying to bring it into accord with our other moral, metaphysical, or scientific beliefs. There is good reason to think that we cannot grasp any teaching this way, however, and the obscure teachings of religious texts are particularly unsuited to it. In any case, the idea that we should be wholly passive listeners to a wholly transparent teaching is *itself* an imposition of a human theory of interpretation on religious texts—a peculiarly modern one, moreover, with nothing to recommend it over the more complex theories of interpretation that held sway over religious communities in the past.

The first choice that religious believers make in receiving revelation concerns simply which parts of their sacred text to read. In every religious community, some parts of a revealed text are well-known while others languish in obscurity. Jews discuss the exodus from Egypt endlessly, and use it as a basis for a great deal of their liturgy, while paying far less attention to the plague of poisonous snakes in the book of Numbers, or anything in the book of Job; Christians play up the aspects of Jesus' teachings that move away from traditional Jewish rituals and pay less attention to passages in which he seems to follow such rituals (e.g. Luke 2:21–24). Jews and Christians nominally share a sacred text but often emphasize different parts of it. Christians read Job, for instance, while Jews read Leviticus and Numbers, which many Christians barely know. These differences are symptomatic of the way the two religious communities, more generally, distinguish themselves from one another.

They also differ, of course, in how they interpret the elements of their shared sacred text that they both read. Even a single religious community may understand its text differently at different times. The moral views it brings to the text may change, for instance, and the moral views it draws from the text will change accordingly. Pacifism was central to early Christianity but virtually disappeared from Christian practice after the conversion of Constantine. Over time, Jewish, Christian, and Muslim communities have each gone through many different attitudes towards the study of "pagan" philosophy, and towards followers of other religions. A defining mark of traditional Jews, Christians, and Muslims in many places today is their hostility to homosexuality, but leading religious figures in all three traditions wrote homoerotic poetry in the Middle Ages.

Again, a religion may be understood very differently by different sub-communities even in the same time period. One group of adherents may translate the text primarily into a set of ceremonies, another into an allegory for philosophical or mystical doctrines, a third into a call for social action. Quakers and Catholics, Hasidim and Conservative Jews, Sufi liberals and Wahhabi sympathizers of al-Qaeda look like they must belong to entirely different religions, even though they regard the same text as sacred.

All these phenomena fall under the heading of how we receive revelation. No text is self-interpreting, and the gnomic, poetic texts that constitute revelation are harder to interpret than most. No moral code is self-applying, and the moral codes embedded in such obscure texts are more difficult to apply than most. A community must therefore have a theory of interpretation—in conjunction, usually, with a moral theory and a theology—if it is to be capable of receiving a revelation. As we have seen, fundamentalists deny this, claiming that their texts wear their meaning on their face, and that any theory about how they should be read is an illegitimate interposition between God's word and the faithful. But, again, this is already a theory about how the texts should be read, a theology and hermeneutics that is as much a human product as the ones that understand sacred texts in philosophical or mystical fashion. A human mode of reception, in response to revelation, is not an option. It is inevitable.

It is also a good thing, religiously. Pace the fundamentalists, the fact that human beings must make decisions about how to understand and implement their revealed texts is not a regrettable necessity, but something integral to revelation—something that God Himself, if He gave these texts, must have intended. Revelation and its reception need each other.

In one sense, this is obvious. If revelation is given, we need to receive it, while if we are engaged in reception, there must be something to receive. Giving and receiving, in all contexts, need each other.

But there is a richer connection between the gift of revelation, specifically, and our reception of that gift. Revelation is angled, obscure, and edgy, speaking to us through its aesthetic properties as much as anything else, and speaking more effectively to some people than to others. But it also purports to be a holistic vision of how all human life can be worthwhile, and in that capacity it should be able to speak to every human being, and enjoin on its followers a path that every human being can recognize as decent and just. The reception of revelation aims to resolve this tension, to transform the angled, quirky vision of the original text into something that can be recognized as a plausible account of the highest human good by all humanity. In receiving revelation, we work to make moral sense of it, and to align it with our independent telic intuitions. This process cannot offer what revelation itself provides—it is not obscure or exciting enough to provide a satisfying vision of our telos—but revelation also does not have the virtues of its reception. They need each other as the beautiful and the moral do in order to compose the highest good. But revelation is supposed to lead us to our highest good. It can do that only if the path it yields is shaped both by a foundational text and by a process in which we actively receive that text.

We need to keep these moments separate. Revelation is given in poetry but received in prose. It is given in poetry because it is essentially mysterious. But something wholly beyond our grasp is not even a mystery—it is merely unknown—and certainly not a mystery in the light of which we can live. So the poetry of revelation must be translated into prose: an attempt, always inadequate, to make clear sense of what it says. Only thereby can the poetry yield a path. To act, to choose a set of practices and plan our participation in them, we need to know their shape in advance, and to do this effectively, and in accordance with morality, the practices need to be integrated into a socially-shared way of life. The reception of revelation makes this possible. It fits a vision of what makes life worth living onto a path that can be shared by a community, and that promotes decency and justice. But it remains a way of *receiving* a revealed vision only so long as it recognizes the asymmetry between its own workings and the revelation to which it responds. Revelation is supposed to provide us with a telic vision that our ordinary ways of thinking cannot provide. It should therefore rupture those ordinary ways of thinking, contrast with them, and show their limits. Accordingly, we receive it *as* revelation only insofar as we recognize the rupture that it makes in our ordinary frameworks. To recognize something as rupturing the way we normally think is, however, simultaneously to recognize that way of thinking as normal, and as ours. What is extraordinary and uncanny in revelation helps us see how important the ordinary and the normal are to us, how much they define us and set limits on what we can take to be true or good. By contrasting with our ordinary ways of thinking, revelation helps us know who we are. And we help it be what it is by accepting it while maintaining our difference from it: by giving it room to teach us.

This last point deserves emphasis. When we interpret revealed texts, we need to preserve their obscurity. The very struggle to bring them in line with our pre-revelatory morality and telic intuitions should force us, again and again, to confront how strange and difficult they are—not to reduce them to something we could have produced by way of our reason alone. But this struggle can actually help promote the sense of strangeness. One who persists in a struggle of this sort, rather than writing off sacred texts as a product of people who lived amidst ancient confusions and biases, is constantly aware that her life is guided by a gnomic wisdom, and not just by her natural faculties.

Revelation and its reception thus belong together by *contrast*; the relationship is lost if we ignore their differences. That is a mistake shared by progressive religious movements and their fundamentalist opponents. Progressive religious movements, over the past two centuries, have come to see sacred scriptures simply as human attempts to grasp God's will; they therefore regard the process of interpreting these texts as continuous with the process by which they were produced. Partly in reaction to this view, some traditionalists have insisted that not just the scriptures themselves but the established pre-modern interpretations of them are direct communications from God, which cannot be challenged in the name of what seems reasonable to us. Both of these views erase the distinction between revelation and its reception. The first dissolves revelation into its reception; the second freezes reception into an additional revelation. But if revelation dissolves into its reception, if the Torah or Gospels or Quran themselves become merely one among many human attempts to grasp what God wants of us, rather than God's own communication to us, then we might as well return to our reason and experience alone as a source for insight into our highest good; there is no reason to suppose that people who lived many centuries before us are likely to have had better insight into that than we do. If the reception of revelation becomes fixed, on the other hand, if we simply submit to our ancestors' attempts to make sense of the Torah, Gospels, or Quran, rather than bringing our own reason and experience to them, then our revealed teachings will effectively become absurd, unconnected with what we ordinarily consider to be good. They will become closed to us, rather than giving us access to a highest good. Revelation, if it takes place at all, must remain beyond us; the reception of revelation, if it is to be a reception, must be in our hands.

This point can be put nicely by way of a distinction that Jews draw between an oral and a written Torah. The oral Torah—the work of the oral teachers known as "rabbis"—is essentially what I have been calling reception. And some rabbis characterize the oral Torah as if it were another fixed text, spoken to Moses at Sinai and passed down intact over the generations: just like the written text except in its mode of transmission. But the core idea behind the notion of an oral Torah is captured better, I think, in the following rabbinic tale:

A non-Jew came before [the famously choleric rabbi] Shammai [and] said to him, "How many Torahs do you have?" He replied, "Two: a written Torah and an oral Torah." Said the non-Jew: "The written Torah I believe in, but the oral Torah I do not believe in. Convert me, on condition that you teach me [just] the written Torah." Shammai rebuked him and drove him away in anger. The non-Jew then came before [the famously gentle rabbi] Hillel who converted him. The first day Hillel taught him the alphabet in the correct order, but the next day he reversed it. The man said to him, "But this isn't what you taught me yesterday." Hillel replied, "Do you not have to depend on me for the letters of the alphabet? So must you . . . depend on me for the interpretation of the Torah."

Here the point is not that a specific oral *content* must accompany the written Torah, but that certain *methods* must be passed down orally along with any written text if it is to be decipherable to future generations. Hillel illustrates the need for this passing down of method by the fact that readers must learn the alphabet orally: which shows neatly, to one who would like to come to God by way of a text alone, how the act of deciphering texts must begin with an oral teaching. But he could have made the same point by appealing to the need to learn the grammar of the language in which the text is written, the rules of inference that the text follows, or how it signals irony and other non-literal language. Or he might have mentioned, if he were philosophically inclined, the fact that a non-naturalistic telic vision must be rendered compatible with the natural needs of believers in each generation if they are to integrate it into their lives, and that an essentially cryptic teaching, like the one Jews attribute to the Torah, must be adjusted to the varying metaphysical and moral views that believers have, over the generations, if they are to recognize it as good.

In any case, a cryptic teaching cries out for figurative interpretation if it is to orient our lives. If revelation functions in our lives like the advice imparted by our friend Aloysius from Chapter 1, we can appreciate its point only when we move away from its most obvious, literal meaning. Consider the story of Joseph and his brothers. Joseph is told in dreams that he will achieve great power over his brothers—but only after both he and the brothers undergo many changes can they wrest a morally decent meaning from that dream-message: a meaning they can plausibly take God to have intended. Similarly, I suggest, the entire Torah, and other claimants to revelation, can come to have a morally decent, plausibly divine meaning for us only if it is brought together with an oral process that adjusts the meaning of the text to the experience of its adherents. The fixed, transcendent text and the flexible, immanent process of oral interpretation illuminate one another. It is in this sense, and this sense only, that they are both essential to God's revelation. As a committed Jew, I think it is true that the written and the oral Torah make up revelation together (were jointly "given at Sinai," as our tradition likes to say). But they belong together in a union of *opposites*, and play sharply different roles in God's communication with us. They need each other but are not alike.

Let's look now at some examples of reception, drawn from the Jewish interpretive tradition since it is the one I know best.

The Torah contains a passage instructing parents with "a stubborn and rebellious son" to bring that son to the elders who hold court at the gates of the city and announce, "This our son is stubborn and rebellious; he will not obey our voice; he is a glutton and a drunkard"; the people of the city are then to stone him to death (Deuteronomy 21:18–21). There could hardly be a more appalling prescription. Like many readers, I cringe when I encounter this passage, and am inclined to draw back from my trust that the Torah reveals a highest good. What can one do if one wants to maintain that trust, and continue to regard the Torah as a font of ethical wisdom? Well, first, as noted in Chapter 4, believers trust a religious text in virtue of the *general telic vision* they find in it, not an inspiration they receive from every verse; in this and other ways religious faith is holistic. So one can, and every Jew today does, stress parts of the text other than these verses, refuse to regard one's own children as "stubborn and rebellious" in the relevant sense, and thereby ignore the passage for all practical intents and purposes. Still, it is hard to see why a text given by God would contain any passage that deserves to be ignored, and it is hard to see how analogical readings, and other tools of non-literal interpretation, can get this passage to yield up an ethically inspiring meaning.

What the rabbis of the Talmud do with the passage is show how it can be used to challenge our very idea of literal interpretation. They suggest that "glutton and drunkard" should be understood such that one could only qualify if one ate the equivalent of an entire ox and drank an entire case of wine. They point out that the son in question would have to be within a very narrow age range. If he is just a child, he is not responsible for his actions (Jewish law, like other legal systems, requires maturity before a person can be held responsible for wrongdoing). But if he is mature enough to be responsible for his actions, he will in most cases be out of his parents' home and control. At the time of the Talmud, he might have had a family of his own by the age of fourteen. So the window in which a law like this might apply must be very narrow: the rabbis decide that it must be a period of a few months right around maturity. Then the rabbis add that for the parents to say that "our son . . . does not obey our voice"—"voice" is singular, in the Hebrew—they must speak with the *same* voice. That is impossible, however: men and women do not have the same kind of voice. So the law cannot be enforced. The rabbis conclude that there never was and never will be a stubborn and rebellious son, in the sense presumed by these verses, and that the point of the passage is not to give law at all but to provide an opportunity for moral teaching. What moral teaching? They don't say explicitly, but perhaps the very teaching that one needs to bring a firm moral compass, and willingness to engage in patient and creative interpretation, to passages as shocking as this one. An apparently immoral command, in the written Torah, thus turns into a source of moral insight in the oral Torah.

Now it is fairly obvious that the rabbis' reading of the text is driven by background moral concerns, although they never expressly say that. Yet the rabbis do not simply *dismiss* the passage as obviously ridiculous or unsuited to religious teaching. Rather, they read it with close attention to its details, pressing its literal sense so hard that it yields up a practical contradiction. They provide, that is, a not implausible set of reasons for understanding the text as *meant*, by God, to provoke in us a reaction that would nullify its apparent prescription, and bring us to the moral reflections that that nullification inspires.

This is one form of reception of a sacred text, not uncommon in pre-modern interpretive traditions. It captures exquisitely the balance that one needs, if one is to draw a moral-beautiful path from an obscure text, between extreme reverence for its details and a creative effort to bring it in line with one's moral intuitions. The rabbis of the Talmud represent this sensibility very well, and use it to soften the implications of many disturbing passages in the Torah. In doing this, they are not acting in bad faith, or substituting their own judgment for what they regard as God's word. Rather, precisely *because* it is God's word, they believe it must be capable of meaning anything that an ingenious and morally-driven human interpreter can come up with.

And this is correct. If one sees a text as produced by a human being, who lived like all human beings in a particular place at a particular time, then the range of its plausible readings will be limited by what someone in that historical context could plausibly have intended. Nothing written by a person who lived in the fifteenth century could be a commentary on Newton's *Principia*, for instance, nor could a first-century Roman writer have exalted the taste of tomatoes. But if the author of a text is supposed to be *God*, history does not limit the range of its meanings. A text God authored can intentionally address me right now, even if it was produced millennia ago. The limits on what God might say are logical and ethical ones, not historical ones. We can understand God's word as addressing any historical epoch. What we cannot do is understand it as intended to teach something ludicrous or evil.

So the rabbis of the Talmud, implicitly following a moral compass, eliminate the law calling for the destruction of stubborn and rebellious sons from Jewish practice. They do something similar elsewhere. The "eye for an eye" passages in the Torah are translated into a tool for determining financial compensation for bodily injury. Capital punishment gets so hedged about with preconditions that Rabbi Eliezer ben Azariah could describe a Sanhedrin who condemned one person to death in seventy years as a bloody Sanhedrin. The rabbis also found ways to ensure that women consented to marriage and had a right to divorce, without any textual basis for such requirements in the Torah. In these and many other respects, rabbinic reception of the Torah softens the harsh demands that the text itself seems to make, and molds its laws into something more respectful of the dignity of every individual—a norm that the text may well contain implicitly but does not explicitly emphasize. The rabbis bring the Torah into line with justice and mercy; they don't simply find those virtues jumping off the page at them.

For the past two millennia, Jewish communities have carried forward this rabbinic reception of the Torah, and over time, it has led to a richly moralized conception of the Torah's laws. On the rabbinic understanding, a whole-hearted pursuit of the path of the Torah will necessarily require and foster virtues of honesty, kindness, and humility. And on the whole, the rabbis interpret Torah law so that it does foster these virtues. That does not mean they produced a tradition that is wholly just or decent. Moral critics of traditional Judaism today often point to its sexism, in particular. Yet there is reason to hope that even this failing can be overcome from within the rabbinic approach. Rabbinic Judaism has already moved Jewish communities far from the sexism that marks the surface level of the Torah. The rabbis of the Talmud introduced laws forbidding marital rape and giving women the right to demand a divorce; recently, traditions keeping women out of Torah study, and leadership positions in the Jewish community, have also begun to change. The process is slow, and hindered by a reactionary backlash that rejects precisely the flexible view of reception that I have defended. But women have achieved enhanced roles even in very traditional circles over the past few decades, and there is reason to expect that this process will continue. And the rabbinic method of interpreting the Torah offers a rich array of resources to further that process.

Both as regards morality and more generally, the Talmud is an outstandingly thoughtful example of how to receive a sacred text. It works verse by verse, however, or law by law; it does not provide grand interpretations of the Torah as a whole. That came later, in the mainstream Jewish tradition, but the philosophers and mystics who engaged in such radical interpretations were inspired, when reading particular passages, by the methods of the Talmud. Maimonides and his followers considered it unintelligible, and conducive to evil, for God to be understood anthropomorphically. They therefore tried to show that every bit of the Bible's anthropomorphic language about God can be understood as metaphorical. The Kabbalists produced almost an opposite view, with a highly anthropomorphic view of God. But both schools employed the same creative techniques for pulling their views out of the text that we saw in the Talmud's account of the stubborn and rebellious son. Indeed, the Kabbalists insisted that *only* this sort of creative reading is appropriate to a sacred text:

> Rabbi Simeon said: Alas for the man who regards the Torah as a book of mere tales and [worldly] matters. If this were so, we might even today write a Torah dealing in such matters and still more excellent.... The tales of the Torah are only her outward garments. If anyone should suppose that the Torah herself is this garment and nothing else, let him give up the ghost. Such a man will have no share in the world to come. That is why David said [Ps 119:18]: "Open thou mine eyes, that I may behold wondrous things out of thy Torah," namely, that which is beneath the garment of the Torah.... [W]hen fools see a man in a garment that seems beautiful to them, they do not look more closely. But more important than the garment is the body, and more important than the body is the soul. So likewise the Torah has a body, which consists of the commandments and ordinances of the Torah, which are called *gufe torah* ["bodies of the Torah": used standardly in rabbinic literature, but not here, to mean what is most important in the Torah]. This body is cloaked in garments, which consist of worldly stories. Fools see only the garment, which is the narrative part of the Torah ... Those who know more see not only the garment but also the body that is under the garment. But the truly wise, the servants of the Supreme King, those who stood at the foot of Mount Sinai, look only upon the soul, which is the true foundation of the entire Torah, and one day indeed it will be given them to behold the innermost soul of the Torah.

On this matter, I think that the Kabbalists are right. The Jewish tradition distinguishes between *pshat*—roughly, "literal" or "straightforward" reading—and *drash*, which literally means "that which has been sought for" and is used to characterize complex, creative modes of interpretation that move far from the surface or straightforward level of the text. Using these terms, I suggest that *drash* is the key to any religious sensibility. If the vision of the highest good held out by a revealed text is necessarily obscure, it follows that the deeper meaning of that text is necessarily *not* something that shows up on its surface. Once we add that such texts are supposed to provide us with a path by which we can transform the aspects of ourselves that keep us from grasping our highest good, it also makes sense that we will learn over time to find deeper meanings in them than we do initially. Aloysius' advisee learns to shift the meaning of the advice he has been given, and to attribute a new meaning to the word "treasure" in the sentence, "There is a treasure in the village over the mountains." In a more complicated story, with a more complicated path to follow, there will be many more shifts, and many more transformations of words. The paths laid out by revealed religions are precisely such complicated paths. What exactly they mean *must* therefore be open, constantly, to imaginative and energetic reinterpretation. Only a believer open to such shifts—open to the sensibility of *drash*—can grasp what a sacred text has to teach him: can allow it to transform him, and find transformed meanings in it when he does.

We may add that sacred texts come into existence at a particular moment in time but are thought to contain a vision that holds across all time. The very idea of revelation, as understood here, entails this. It entails that a particular set of words, somewhat obscure to us when we first hear it, can guide us to our telos if we trust it, and try in the light of the path it opens for us to understand it better. But that means that the telic teaching we trust must be enshrined in the particular words, uttered or written at a particular time, that we take to reveal it, even as our understanding of those words shifts over time. It is in this sense that revealed religion is necessarily *historical* (it is often called "historical religion" instead of revealed religion). The original utterance regarded as revealed—the Torah or Vedas or sayings of the Buddha—must be couched in terms that make sense to its listeners at the time, but those terms will not make the same sense to later listeners. On the simplest of levels, the Buddha brings examples from the way chariots work, and the Torah talks about ancient modes of dress that have long ceased to exist. Ancient texts like these also presuppose modes of worship or marriage that are radically different from those of later generations. If these aspects of the text are still to speak to later believers—as they must, if the author of the text is God, or a human being with supernatural insight into all of nature—those later believers must reinterpret them, and assume that their meaning was meant, by their supernatural author, to shift over time. Maimonides suggested that God accommodated himself to the idolatrous tendencies of the Israelite people by allowing them to worship Him by way of sacrifice—that the Torah means to wean the Israelites from their idolatrous tendencies by re-directing sacrifice from the service of many gods to the service of the one Creator. Some modern Jews argue that the sexist tendencies of the Torah can be understood as a similar accommodation, and that Judaism can now move away from them as it has moved away from sacrifice. How exactly to understand "accommodation," and what its limits might be, is a vexed question that I shall not try to answer. But a God who reveals His will for us must do so from within the norms of the culture that receives His revelation, even if He wants that culture to change: it will not understand Him otherwise. This reinforces the centrality of *drash* to the sensibility of those who receive revelation. Receivers must assume that the meaning of what they have been taught will shift as their values shift, that it was spoken in one way to people who lived at one time, and its meaning for later generations will necessarily be somewhat different.

Which is to say that God himself, if He reveals Himself in a text, must want us to engage in *drash*. The rabbis declare that "the Torah speaks in the language of man": that in authoring the Torah, God Himself employed the quirks and colloquialisms of a language like Hebrew. This is a daring theological presumption. Why would the eternal Being, the source and structuring principle of the entire universe, express himself in a particular, historical human language? Wouldn't such a Being speak, if He spoke at all, in a perfect language that any thinking creature anywhere could understand—a language that *transcends* "the language of man"? There is a paradox here very much like the one that Christians see in the idea of God becoming human; the idea of God speaking *is*, indeed, a form of "incarnation." Yet the paradoxical claim is true—so devout Jews and Christians believe at least. Indeed, they regard belief in this paradox as crucial to their religions. A religion with paradox at its core, however, needs constant reinterpretation—constant *drash*. So God, if He deliberately appears in a paradoxical way, as He must if He appears historically, must want us to engage in *drash*.

We may add that in struggling to pull an eternal and universal meaning out of a historically located text, we model the sort of ethical relationship that all human beings, religious or secular, need to have with their communities. On the one hand, we owe duties of affection, gratitude, and loyalty to the people with whom we share a community. On the other hand, we have duties to all humanity that transcend our duties to our communities. Notoriously, these different demands on us—the call of belonging on the one hand and the call of humanism on the other— can conflict with one another. In negotiating a path between them, we generally find that we need to work *within* our community's established ways of living even as we try to open those ways to new ideas. We appeal to one aspect of our shared norms as part of our case for revising other aspects of those norms; we try in any case both to honor our community and to transcend it. Meanwhile, a decent community will urge changes on its individual members in the same way: displaying a respect for their habits and established interests even as it tries to alter them. So individuals and their communities are engaged in a constant process of moving between where they are historically and where they aspire to be ethically—precisely the struggle that a person committed to a revealed religion needs to engage in as regards her sacred text. And as they engage in this process, their ethical language changes; their interpretation of their basic moral and political texts changes accordingly. The very process of reaching for ethical standards that transcend history, that stand beyond the standards we happen to have at a particular moment, thus requires that we allow the meaning of authoritative texts, whether secular or sacred, to shift over time.

I have begun to emphasize the place of community in reception. Reception is first and foremost an individual task—no text will *be* a revelation to me unless *I* take it on as such—but revelation is fully received only in community. This, for two reasons. First, in order to be humbled by a text, I need to check my understanding of it against that of other people. Otherwise I am likely to massage it so that it tells me only what I want to hear, and wind up following the dictates of my own desires and beliefs. Only by submitting to the guidance of others can I truly open myself to a teaching from beyond me. Second, what I am supposed to get from this text is an orienting point for all my activity. But almost all my actions are shared with others. I raise children with others; I work with and for others; most of my entertainment I get from others or share with others; and I can protect and enhance my neighborhood only together with others. If my telic vision affects none of these activities, it can hardly affect my life. And if it does affect these activities, then it perforce delineates a distinctive way of being social, of having a community, and anyone committed to the revelation will and should seek out a community with others who share that commitment. Revelations thus call on their adherents to form communities, to bring their teachings into a social way of living.

It is no accident, then, that the path of every revealed religion consists largely in communally-shared practices. To a considerable extent, indeed, communal practice shapes the path far more than the revealed text does. Revealed texts often do not expressly lay out much of a path. The Torah has laws touching every domain of human life, but the New Testament largely inveighs *against* this law-governed conception of life.

And the *Tao te Ching* is written in an ethereal manner that disdains practical prescriptions. Yet the religions associated with all three of these texts have detailed ritual disciplines. Christians take certain of Jesus' actions to gesture towards a path they should follow. He ate bread and drank wine at the Last Supper, so a stylized eating of bread and drinking of wine became a central act for Christian communities. A form of prayer he recommended became integral to Christian liturgy, and his birth and death are commemorated in major holidays. Specifically Christian modes of marriage and burial have also been developed, as well as ceremonies to mark birth and entrance into the Christian community. The New Testament itself does not prescribe any of these things (it does hint at communion), but if one is to develop specifically Christian ways of praying, affirming community with fellow believers, and marking life-cycle events, these seem as reasonable as any.

Moreover, for all the differences between Christianity and Judaism, *halacha*—the path that Jews draw from the Torah—has developed in quite a similar way. To be sure, explicit ritual commands take up far more space in the Torah than in the Gospels, but the practices Jews derive from their sacred text differ considerably from what it explicitly says, and include many rituals that are nowhere to be found in it. The Torah mandates some sort of abstention from work on the seventh day of the week, but it took an elaborate process of interpretation to establish what exactly that means. The Torah says nothing about how one ought to conduct a marriage ceremony, but Jewish tradition—judging, reasonably, that a religious path ought to mark events like this—has constructed such a ceremony. And Jewish liturgy, like Christian liturgy, draws heavily on elements in the Hebrew Scriptures, but doesn't restrict itself to the explicit prayers to be found there.

So the connection between a revelation and a practical path needn't be made by the revealed text itself; it may instead be developed by the community of that text's adherents, as they try to incorporate its teachings into their way of life. To some extent, a communal process indeed dominates the practice of every revealed religion. To integrate a revealed teaching into the ongoing practices of our lives, which are overwhelmingly defined by our societies, and to ensure that the telic vision of that teaching coheres with morality, we need a community of like-minded believers. In this sense, reception by a community is essential to revelation: it cannot shape our lives otherwise.

But that is not to say that reception is *only* a communal matter. At the end of the day, each of us has to take responsibility for our own individual lives, and we accept telic visions, if we do, because we believe, as individuals, that they make best sense of the overall worth or point of those lives. Indeed, I separated the telic off from the moral aspects of ethics in Chapter 2 precisely because morality is directed to the needs of a community and for that reason is unable to settle the question of what gives our individual lives a meaning or point. Revelation comes in first and foremost to fulfill this individual need, and religious community enters the picture only because individuals need to work together if they are to translate those revealed visions into practice. The fact that our religious communities are in the end a means to the realization of a vision we accept as individuals entails that we can never renounce our responsibility to make sure that that vision coheres with our individual moral and telic intuitions. What we take from our religious communities must make sense to us as individuals. It is always possible that our community has gone wrong, has become corrupted or deluded or otherwise fallen prey to the tendencies that, according to our religious vision itself, bar human beings from grasping their highest good with their natural faculties alone. A Jew must constantly worry about the possibility that his community has fallen into idolatry; a Christian, that it has moved away from Christ; a Hindu, that it has retreated into *maya*.

Our religious communities are thus not like our political communities or our families: imposed on us by law, or given to us by natural feeling. Rather, insofar as we are religious, we choose them and shape them, and are obligated by our religious commitment itself to leave them or try to alter them if we think they have gone wrong. Religious communities are and should be shaped by the individual choices of their members, even as the communities also shape those members' choices. In practice, the individual role in shaping communities shows up when people move from one type of community to another (become a Reform instead of an Orthodox Jew, for instance, or vice versa), or convert to a different religion, or start or join dissident movements ("heresies") within their community. Less drastically, some people simply adjust their practice—making it stricter or more lenient, more oriented to prayer or to study, more mystical or more concerned with practical human needs. All of these possibilities bring out the fact that reception is individual as well as communal, and that there is a complex, dynamic interplay between the two.

I have given examples of reception from the Jewish tradition, but the points I have made hold just as much for other religions. The differences between rationalist and mystical versions of Islam are vast, but both grow out of shared traditions about how to interpret the Quran, as do the various schools of Islamic law, and modern movements to reform Islam in more liberal directions or purify it of liberal tendencies. In the hands of Meister Eckhart and Teresa of Avila, Christian Scripture looks very different than it does in the hands of Thomas Aquinas, and it looks yet different in the hands of Luther, Calvin, George Fox, or John Wesley. All represent ways of receiving the same Christian text, however, and all have shaped communities of like-minded believers who pursue a path that accords with their way of interpreting that text. Much the same goes on in Buddhist communities—think of the differences between Theravada and Mahayana Buddhism, or the differences, within the latter, between Tibetan and Japanese practices. In all cases, reception combines a way of interpreting texts with modes of practice, and of forming and maintaining communities. No text can have an impact on our lives without this process, and no text can have an ongoing influence on our lives unless the process is fluid, responding to differences in the circumstances and outlook of a community across time. So if God has given any group of human beings a text that is supposed to shape their lives across time, God must have meant for that text to be accepted, and passed down, in a fluid process of reception.

Exactly what religious function reception serves may however be understood differently in different traditions. Jews can readily characterize the importance of reception by saying that God wants us to receive His word autonomously. The Torah repeatedly indicates that God values human autonomy. Abraham calls God Himself to account by asking whether He really intends to sweep away the wicked together with the innocent in Sodom: "That be far from You! Shall not the judge of all the world do justly?" (Genesis 18:25). Moses also argues with God, as do Jonah and Job, and Jacob wrestles with God. From this perspective, the morally challenging aspects of the Torah, like the passage about the stubborn and rebellious son, can be regarded as invitations from God to interpret His words autonomously. We may even say that one *purpose* of revelation is to provoke us into free, creative interpretation. The moral challenges in the text, the marks of the Torah's cultural embeddedness that need to be reinterpreted over time, are grains of sand that have occasioned the pearl of the rich interpretive tradition in Judaism. By way of these challenges in the text, we may say, God summons Jews to work along with Him in playing out the telic vision He has provided them.

But other traditions may prefer a different understanding of reception. For Muslims, perhaps the need for human beings to work out for themselves what God means in the Quran is a way for them to experience their submission to God's will more deeply. For Christians, the receptive process may be an expression of their gratitude for salvation. For Buddhists, it may be a way for people to re-work their customary ways of thought so that they truly grasp, rather than simply mouth, the teachings that bring enlightenment. The particular understanding each tradition holds of why revelation must be actively received, and what that reception amounts to, is itself part of their receptive process, and will differ in accordance with their different telic visions. But no tradition can honestly maintain that revelation is self-interpreting, or presented transparently to wholly passive believers. Reception is an active process, by which we human beings shape the revealed teachings we believe we have been given, on any plausible view of what revelation can accomplish.

It is important to keep the religious reception of revelation separate from the historical study of purportedly revealed texts. One who receives a text as religious revelation sees it as embodying a divine, or at any rate superhuman, wisdom, however much free and creative interpretation it may take to pull out that wisdom. One who regards such a text purely as the product of a human being or group of human beings is looking, by contrast, precisely for what it meant *to* that person or group of people in their time and place. This does not mean that historians of religious texts cannot be religious, but it does mean that they take up a radically different stance toward their text when they treat it religiously than they do when they study it historically, and that they should not expect their historical work to be particularly helpful to them religiously.

A religious person can grant quite readily, I think, that his or her sacred text was produced by various human beings, with all their limitations. A Jew need not deny, for instance, that the sources known by historical scholars of the Bible as J, E, P, H, and D wrote the Torah rather than Moses. But for a religious Jew—one committed to receiving her telos from the Torah—God must have worked *through* these human authors, and must be the ultimate author of the Torah, no matter how it came into existence historically. Only then will she have any inclination to humble herself to the text, to presume that it contains a wisdom beyond her own even when it seems mistaken or confused—to presume that she, rather than it, is mistaken or confused. A historian cannot humble his judgment to the moral or telic beliefs of the people he studies, however, or reject the possibility that those people were mistaken or confused. A historian cannot even *identify* the worldview of J or P unless he looks for the interests or prejudices that mark that author off from other people, and align him or her with the opinions shared by a particular culture or sub-culture, at a particular time and place. This can be very interesting, and a religious believer may be as fascinated as anyone else by such historical details. But *as* religious believer—as a believer, more precisely, in the revealed religion defined by this text—it makes no sense for her to guide her life by the text unless it represents a telic wisdom that transcends time and place. Why on earth should I suppose that some ancient Israelite courtier or priest, beset by all the errors and biases of his time and place, had insight into the highest good that I am not capable of myself? I trust the authors of the Torah because I think that they spoke for *God*, not for themselves, and because I trust God's wisdom to far transcend my own, such that I can hope to grasp it, even in part, only if I first try faithfully to follow it. But that is to say that the Torah is transformed for me when I treat it as revelation (transformed into something that can transform me), and that that attitude towards it is incompatible with treating it as a mere historical product, on par with other human writings. James Kugel—a historical scholar of the Hebrew Bible who is also a religious Jew—puts this point beautifully:

The person who seeks to learn *from* the Bible is smaller than the text; he crouches at its feet, waiting for its instructions or insights. Learning *about* the text generates the opposite posture. The text moves from subject to object; it no longer speaks but is spoken about, analyzed, and acted upon. The insights are now all the reader's, not the text's and anyone can see the results.

I don't mean to rule out all possibility that historical study can illuminate a religious text. Sometimes knowing more about how the words of a passage were used in their ancient context may help me see a meaning in it that I can comfortably attribute to God. But it will be coincidence when this happens. It is no more likely that I will find deeper telic insight into the text by way of historical study than by applying a Kantian, Freudian, or Marxist framework to it. Some theologians have put more stock than this in the historical study of sacred texts. They however have tended to see the progress of history as itself a form of revelation. Hegel defended such a view, and he influenced a long line of theologians who understood the Hebrew Bible and the New Testament as stages in a process of revelation that continues into our own day. It is clear why someone with this view might consider studying their sacred text as an historical artifact to be essential to the proper reception of revelation. Most of us, however, regard history as a much more haphazard business, with no clear philosophical significance, and for us it is hard to see why figuring out the concatenation of accidents that, say, led a group of priests in Judea to compose parts of Genesis and Numbers, should be of any value in determining our highest ideals.

In summary, we may say that the reception of a revealed text needs to draw out from it a communally usable, morally admirable, and spiritually inspiring way of living, that is at the same time reflective enough of the literal level of the text for us to be able, in good faith, to regard ourselves as following that text. A sincere and thoughtful reception, determined to pull out from its cryptic source something that believers can accept as a vision of the highest good, will thus consist in a delicate balance between considerations that accommodate the source to independent demands of human reason and considerations that keep believers humbled to the super-human insight they attribute to the text. The very nature of revelation demands that reception walk this delicate line: that it both graft onto and transcend our independent beliefs about goodness.

Reception must also be communal while at the same time making sense to each individual believer. It must be communal because it must yield a path that individuals can pursue together with others, and because humbling oneself to a community is the most direct and forceful way of achieving humility more generally. But it must make sense to each individual as well if the community is not to stray from its vision and or allow its authority to become a vehicle for the personal agendas of the community's leaders.

In addition, reception must be traditional—passed down (*traditio*) by each generation of believers to the next—while at the same time adjusting to the different needs of people who live in different places and times. It must be traditional for much the same reasons that it must be communal: because a community can only maintain a path over time if there is considerable continuity between what it does in one generation and what it does in the next, and because communities can best humble themselves to a teaching beyond themselves if they check their modes of interpretation against those of their ancestors. But reception must at the same time respond to the new needs, discoveries, and shifts in outlook of each generation, if it is to reflect the understanding of that generation. So a sincere and thoughtful reception will balance deference to the past against sensitivity to the present just as it balances a respect for community against a respect for the individuals comprising that community, and a respect for the rational conditions on revelation against a respect for the elements of revelation that transcend rationality.

All these balances are hard to pin down precisely. There are certainly no hard-and-fast rules to determine what good interpretation should look like. The philosopher Ludwig Wittgenstein argued convincingly that rules cannot fix the interpretation of any kind of speech. Any rule to guide interpretation would itself have to be interpreted, after all, and if we find a rule to guide *that* rule's interpretation, the new rule will in turn have to be interpreted ... Interpretation, whether it concerns religious texts or not, is thus a process that we cannot, even in principle, pin down precisely. Nevertheless, any community sharing a practice of interpretation will declare that some interpretations are close to the text and others far from it; some fit in with the community's general vision and ideals while others betray that vision; some are clever or deep and others silly or shallow. We make judgments of this sort whenever we engage in legal or literary interpretation, and members of a community that shares a practice of legal or literary interpretation can agree readily on many such judgments—agree at least that certain interpretations are plausible, others a stretch, and still others so outlandish that they do not count as interpretations at all. We *must* agree in many such judgments else we could not form communities of interpretation: could not share ways of applying laws or reading literature. That was in fact Wittgenstein's point: that shared interpretation goes on by way of shared communal practices

even in the absence of rules that might ground it. But believers committed to the same religious text are just one instance of an interpretive
community. They must be able to achieve some sort of consensus in
judgment, therefore, even if their way of interpreting their texts cannot
be deduced from a rule.

And individual believers come to or move away from a particular
interpretive community in accordance with their individual judgment
about what constitutes good judgment. We all use our judgment, among
other things, to ascertain whether others have good judgment—that is
what guides us toward some literary and legal communities and away
from others. Once again, religious judgment is just an instance of this
more general phenomenon. Believers judge whether a particular way of
interpreting their sacred text is in good faith, and thereby gravitate
towards some communities of fellow believers and away from others.

Three implications of the account of reception I have given:

First, it is essential, pace those who think that God should communicate in crystal-clear ways, that revelation be *un*clear, that what it means
cannot be fully available on its surface. Revelations are essentially mysterious, and we must preserve the mystery in them if we believe that the
good they present is something we cannot find with our natural faculties
alone. One consequence is that no moment of reception will ever be
wholly adequate to the revelation it is trying to take in; the process of
reception goes on endlessly. That is as it should be. If the promise of
holiness is that we will forever be able to find the world fascinating—new,
unexpected, mysterious—then it is essential to revelation that it never be
comprehensive, never show on its surface all the goodness it promises.
There is a tension between the completeness of the good that is supposed
to be revealed and the need for that good to promise a recurrence of the
unexpected or new. We resolve that tension by understanding our
revealed texts as offering us a full good only over time: as unfolding
their true meaning, not at a single moment, but over the entire time,
perhaps an infinite one, in which we regard them as our guide. The initial
moment of revelation is one in which we get just a hint or glimpse of our
highest good. That is enough to get us to embark on a path that returns
us continually, with greater understanding, to the vision we glimpsed.
That is enough, also, to get us to wrestle with our source of revelation
interpretively—which is itself part of why we find it beautiful, part of

what inspires us to love it, and its vision of our lives. So the holiness, the moral-beautiful power, of revelation comes out fully only when we try to live out its implications, and struggle with what it means. We might say: the revelation itself needs continually to be revealed. Or, less paradoxically: the revelatory text, the source of revelation, becomes full revelation only in the endless process of reception. An eternal being can speak to us across time, so if God is the source of our revealed text, then we can see God as speaking to us, through that text, in every generation.

It should therefore be clear, also—this is the second implication—that the reception of a revelation will vary from community to community. The meaning and practical path people draw from a teaching meant to present their highest good will of necessity vary in accordance with their different moral ideals, and theories of metaphysics and interpretation. It therefore makes perfect sense that some Jews will be rationalists and some mystics, that some Christians will find Aquinas, others Luther or Calvin, their best key to the mysteries of their sacred text. And it makes sense that these various Jews and Christians, like Sufi and non-Sufi Muslims, or Vaishnava and Shaivite Hindus, will form different sorts of communities within their traditions. A God, or supernaturally wise human being, who reveals our highest goal to us would have to expect that we will receive Her word in these different ways. Insofar as God wants the best for us, God must indeed *want* our understanding of Her words to vary in this way.

Finally, it should be clear that the variety and fluidity essential to reception allows for all the moral progress that liberal religious believers want to achieve, as regards their traditions' faith and practices. There is no need to emend the revealed or sacred texts central to Judaism, Christianity, or Islam, or to demote them from their sacred status and declare them a mere artifact of human history. If a sacred text is supposed to reveal the highest good for all humanity, then it must be able to reflect our highest moral ideals. If God, or a supernaturally wise human being, is its source, then its significance must transcend history, and be able to incorporate whatever we now take to be essential to the good, not just what was seen that way when it was written. So the process of reception, the process by which we interpret and implement our sacred texts, can bring out these ideals even where the text itself, on its surface, does not. And in fact, this ahistorical and moralized approach to sacred texts has long shaped their reception in religious communities across the world.

As noted earlier, both friends and foes of revealed religion tend today to ignore or deny the importance of reception. The different ways in which sacred texts are interpreted or implemented seems to our historically-minded world a mere addition to those texts, projecting back on to them the beliefs of later generations and distorting their "real" meaning—which, it is assumed, must be the meaning they had for their initial writers or readers. Traditional religious believers hold the same historicist view, but claim either that the meaning of their texts is transparent or that their community was given a specific mode of interpreting its text, along with the text itself, by God. Against both these views I have argued that a rich, fluid process of reception is essential to bringing out the good in revelation—and is, in any case, inevitable. Every generation and every community uses its moral and scientific understanding of the world to receive the text or teaching it takes to be revealed. The question is just whether it recognizes that it is doing that.

Revelation is not given until it is received, and its giver, if all-wise, must have known that. It follows that the multifarious human attempts to make sense of sacred texts must themselves be *part* of revelation, not a mere accompaniment to it, let alone a betrayal of it. In giving due respect to the reception of revelation, we are *inter alia* restoring something essential to revelation itself. Only via its reception—which is to say, its many, varied, fluid reception*s*, in the various communities that are committed to it—can a revealed vision acquire significance for us: can it orient and shape our lives.

7

Diversity and Respect

If there are a variety of receptions, for each revelation, might there also be a variety of revelations? Or is there just one true revelation? And if there is one true revelation—one correct vision of the highest good for all humanity—what should we say about the human beings who don't accept that vision? Are they damned, or doomed to endless suffering, or at any rate less than fully good human beings? Or might they be saved in spite of themselves, or capable of a fully good life, even though they don't grasp what the fully good life looks like? These are the questions of religious diversity, and I would like to close this book with a few reflections on them.

People committed to one revealed religion may hold many different attitudes towards adherents of other religions, and toward the non-religious. They may believe there is no way to achieve the highest human good outside of their own religion; they may see elements of what they consider the true way to holiness or enlightenment in many traditions but regard their own as the best; or they may regard many other traditions as just as true (trustworthy) as their own. Some people claim to take up a yet more radically pluralist position, on which *all* religions are equally good or true. Most philosophers and theologians think that this position is incoherent, however, and I am inclined to agree. If one sets out to regard all religions as equally good or true, after all, what does one say about a tradition that insists that its way is the only right one? One will surely have to reject at least that aspect of this tradition, and regard traditions that themselves avow greater pluralism as better for doing so. This already vitiates the project of seeing all traditions as *equally* good or true. In addition, one will have to decide what counts as a religious tradition at all (should we count Jim Jones' violent cult of the 1970s?; how about scientologists, who don't regard themselves as a religion, or followers of Lyndon LaRouche?) and in doing so, will inevitably smuggle in judgments about what religions should accomplish.

In practice, few people respect all religions equally. Even those who trumpet their radical pluralism tend to condemn Jim Jones' cult and other oppressive and violent groups. Most people who gravitate towards the pluralistic end of the spectrum are instead concerned to affirm the equal decency or reasonableness of the world's major, long-standing religions—Judaism, Christianity, Taoism, etc.—along perhaps with the practices of aboriginal peoples. Most pluralists are *limited* pluralists, we might say, seeking a basis on which to value as many religious communities as they can, while limiting that set to groups that keep to certain moral standards.

There are in addition at least two quite different ways of enacting pluralism: tolerance and respect. We tolerate people we consider wrong-headed and shallow, but we don't respect them. Respect involves more than toleration. We have respect for something only if we think that it has features we admire and from which we can learn. Consequently, while tolerating religions one finds contemptible is a not insignificant political achievement—many parts of the world would be freer and more peaceful if everyone held that attitude—full-blown pluralists usually urge *respect* for a variety of religious traditions, not mere toleration. In the rest of this chapter, I will reserve the word "pluralism" for views on which we have reason to respect other traditions. Views that urge mere toleration are compatible with the belief that one's own tradition is the only right one—with a monistic rather than a pluralistic view of religious truth.

But how can a religious person justify either toleration or respect for other religions? Well, even if one considers one's own religion to be the only correct one, one may believe that everyone must come to the truth about God, or about the point of human life, on his or her own. And someone who believes this may strive earnestly to persuade others of the vision she has accepted, or to present it in an attractive light, while opposing the use of coercion to bring people into her faith. This is a common route to toleration.

For respect, we need more. One may respect another religious tradition out of cognitive humility. One may think, "Even if my religion seems to me the best or only right one, I should keep myself open to the possibility that I could be wrong." Or one may believe that a supremely good and loving God couldn't possibly have allowed large numbers of people to come to wholly false or evil beliefs about Him, so the core of one's own religious beliefs must show up in other traditions as well. More radically, one may believe that a supremely good God must have ensured that some unique aspect of the good for humanity is revealed in each (morally decent) religious tradition: that one's own tradition can and should, therefore, learn from the worldviews of all the others.

The account of revealed religion developed in this book can support both monistic and pluralistic views. If the visions presented by our revelations are obscure, and if a criterion of their plausibility is that they lead us to love our lives, we have some reason to favor pluralism. Regarding my religious teaching as obscure gives me reason for cognitive humility. And regarding my religious commitment as dependent centrally on the love for my life it induces in me gives me reason to expect that other people will be inspired to religious commitment by different visions: people love in very different ways, after all. In addition, the idea that an obscure God might reveal different aspects of His or Her will or nature to different people makes good sense. It is indeed not implausible that an obscure and loving God would expect all of us to learn from one another's traditions and thereby to respect one another. So all three modes of respect I have listed, all three reasons for religious pluralism, can gain support from my account of revealed religion.

But if the vision of the highest good disclosed by a revealed text is obscure, that may also mean that lurking within its teaching are reasons why one can achieve that good only by committing oneself to *this* particular text, and the tradition associated with it. Perhaps one's faith will eventually enable one to see that other traditions are, of necessity, confused or distorted. Moreover, the fact that the vision in each of these texts is supposed to be of the highest good for all humanity gives us some reason to suppose that there can in the end be only one right text. When drawn to a revealed religion, on my account, we presume that there is an objective answer to the question, "what makes life worth living?" But that entails that the answer to the question must be an answer for human beings in general, not just for ourselves. Of course there will have to be room in any such answer for different people to lead different kinds of life—society would collapse if everybody had to be an artist or philosopher or politician—but we might need to consult a single telos for all humanity even to figure out how to differentiate our lives. Accordingly, the idea that everyone ought to, say, have faith in Christ or grasp the Buddha's teaching of selflessness is not implausible. Religious traditions need not make such monistic claims, but nothing in my account of religion rules them out.

I think that people are generally drawn to a particular religious revelation in part because they are *already* monists or pluralists, and they see this text or teaching as favoring their view. They are also likely to interpret their tradition, where it is ambiguous, in accordance with their monism or pluralism. Personally, I see the Jewish tradition as quite pluralistic—holding up the Torah as the best expression of what God wants for all humanity, but allowing that other religions may also provide their followers with a godly path—and am committed to it in part for that reason. Someone who thinks that religion should lay out the one right path for everybody might be drawn to Christianity or Buddhism instead, since those traditions have standardly seen themselves as the single correct religion for everyone. Our monistic or pluralistic predilections are one of the many factors contributing to the holistic judgment we make about the trustworthiness of a particular religious tradition. Sometimes the tradition to which we commit ourselves also *leads* us to a more monistic or pluralistic outlook. There is a circle here, although not a vicious one, between the judgments that bring us to religious commitment and the way that that commitment shapes our judgments. But the philosophical account of religion I have delineated contributes little to these judgments: it cannot settle the question of whether we should be pluralists or monists. Whether there are many good religious traditions or just one belongs among the questions about the human good that gets settled by each revealed tradition in a different way, not by the framework that explains what these traditions are trying to accomplish in general.

Nevertheless, it is easy to see how the framework I have developed can be used to buttress a pluralistic view of religion. The emphasis in that framework on the need for telic visions to inspire love and awe in us does make pluralism seem better suited to it than monism. We might expect *reason* to lead us to just one religious view, but if our religious views depend on *love*, they are likely to vary. In addition, one important motivation for my framework is to show how an acceptance of revealed religion can be combined with a commitment to liberal morality, and a heavy dose of pluralism—of respect for the different ways people choose to live—generally goes along with liberal morality. Accordingly, it would not be surprising if people who accept my framework generally use it to support a pluralistic reading of their tradition. I myself am inclined in that direction, and although I will need to go beyond philosophical considerations to defend this inclination, and draw as well on my personal religious beliefs, let me take a few moments to sketch how even a believer who endorses a revealed, traditional religion might be a pluralist.

The Torah repeatedly admonishes Jews to "teach their children" various central aspects of our religion (Genesis 18:19; Exodus 12:26, 13:8, 14; Deuteronomy 6:7, 20–25, 11:19). Which makes good sense. Our first bond of love is normally with our parents, they are the first people to care for us, and God is supposed to be the ultimate source of love and care: God reaches us in revelation by way of love and leads us, through revelation, to love our lives. So it makes good sense for God to urge us to pass down the teachings of revelation through the parent-child bond. We come, if we do, to a vision of God's end for us, and the path to that end, by way of an affective commitment. One of the religious visions in the world speaks to us: which is to say it arouses love in us, offers satisfaction to our telic yearnings. But the yearnings that we have, and the love that satisfies them, will depend on the circumstances in which we were raised and in which our affective dispositions were shaped: including, prominently, our relationship to our parents. It is therefore no surprise that the vision that generally speaks most profoundly to us is a vision presented in our families; the love we feel for it is, initially, an extension of our love for our parents.

Nor should it be a surprise that our religious commitments tend also to be shaped by the larger culture to which our family belongs. It is in the context of that culture, after all, that we normally have, and interpret, the experiences on the basis of which we yearn for a vision that would make our lives worth living. The answer to the telic questions we ask will make best sense to us if couched in the vocabulary of the culture in which we asked those questions; and our love for that answer—the basis on which we accept it—will be in part an extension of our love for our community.

And again, it should not be surprising that a loving God might allow us to develop our religious commitments in this way. If God must speak in human language in order to express His will to us, then why should God not also have to work through the patterns of human love in order to express His love for us? Indeed, these are just intellectual and emotional versions of the same thing. We can grasp the ultimate end God holds out to us intellectually only through parables and prescriptions couched in ordinary human language, and we can grasp that end emotionally only through the modes of affection by which we commit ourselves to ordinary human relationships. God must speak through human emotional formations, through the patterns of love and commitment we develop in our families and cultures, just as He must speak through human linguistic formations. They are not, indeed, sharply separable. And the God I personally believe in—the God who places honoring parents in the first tablet of the Ten Commandments, who repeatedly emphasizes the need for parents to teach the Torah to their children, and who makes remembering the history of one's people essential to religious commitment—seems expressly to recognize, and to want us to recognize, that faith is not primarily an exercise of individual reason or feeling, but a response to and development of the modes of love taught in a family and a culture. It would follow, as most of the Jewish tradition has held, that this same God will relate to people in different cultures through teachings other than the Torah, that God's vision for them is different from God's vision for the Jews.

But so far I have justified only toleration. What I have said enables me to see other religions as on the same level as my own, but not to think that they have anything to offer me, anything from which I can learn. Is there anything in the Jewish tradition to encourage *respect* for other traditions?

Well, one intriguing feature of the revelation at Sinai is the fact that it comes about immediately after Moses takes advice from his non-Israelite father-in-law Jethro—a priest of Midian—about sharing his authority with others. (Indeed, the section of the Torah in which the revelation at Sinai takes place is known as "Jethro" in the Jewish tradition.) Is it too far-fetched to say that only this decentralization of authority makes possible revelation to the whole people—and that it took an outsider to see that? Jethro is a wonderful model of a non-Jew from whom Jews can learn, religiously: a sympathetic onlooker, who can see what we, immersed in our set ways, cannot see, and help us better achieve our own aims. So we may take a hint from a central moment in our own Torah that there is much about human relations that we can learn—*must* learn—from people outside our tradition.

There is an even stronger hint of such an idea in the biblical book of Jonah (read on Yom Kippur, our holiest day), where the Assyrians serve as a model of repentance for Jews. Something similar goes for the book of Ruth (also read on a central religious holiday), where a member of the much-despised Moabite people is held up as a model of decency, generosity, and loyalty. And the Talmud contains the beautiful admonition, "Despise no person and no thing, for every person has his hour and every thing has its place" (Avot 4:3), which I have heard quoted by extremely devout Jews to justify respect for atheists. Atheists have their "hour" in the doing of works of kindness, since their very lack of belief in God can lead them to focus more intensely than believers do on the needs of their fellow human beings.

All my examples thus far, unsurprisingly, are of cases in which Jews learn something of *moral* value from people outside their tradition. In any religious tradition, it is more likely that one will look outside that tradition for moral than for telic insight. It is the telic insights of a religious tradition that distinguish it, after all, and to which the faith for which it calls is directed. Morality is something we share for the most part with all human beings. Accordingly, we may expect to learn more about it from people in any religious tradition. We do not expect the same as regards our distinctively religious beliefs.

Nevertheless, other traditions do sometimes teach us ways of interpreting our own telic vision that we would not otherwise have encountered. I have learned a lot about prayer from the moving spontaneous benedictions I have heard Christian friends offer. On a communal level, Jews and Christians learned from the merger of Aristotle and revealed religion first carried out by Muslims; in a later day Kant profoundly shaped how Jews came to understand their tradition; recently, elements of Hindu and Buddhist practice have had an impact on many American religious communities. These borrowings are possible because we come to our various telic visions for much the same sorts of reasons—a desire to order our goals, a fear of emptiness and death, a belief that lives devoted to pleasure alone will be empty—and we make use of similar metaphysical and moral frameworks to interpret those visions. So even while each of us finds one of these visions more inspiring, moving, etc. than the others, and/or sees it as better suited to his or her particular experience of what makes for a meaningful or empty life, we share the idea that these are the right *sorts* of reasons to ground a religious commitment. We can therefore illuminate one another's understanding of these reasons. Even if I don't share a Christian's understanding of Jesus' Passion, I may be able to see something of value in the idea of vicarious suffering, and use that idea to interpret elements of my own tradition. Even if I don't share a Buddhist's view of the value in meditation, I may learn something from the idea of clearing one's mind of distracting thoughts, or dwelling in the present moment, and therefore incorporate a version of meditation into my own religious practice.

Religions can thus learn from one another while retaining their integrity: they can uphold their visions as the best overall conception of the good human life while still respecting one another. Even insofar as they *disagree*, moreover, they can see each other as valuable correctives to themselves. Each religious tradition should recognize that other traditions serve as an excellent check on how it is living up to its norms of action and interpretation. The criticisms of Jewish practice long made by Christians and Muslims, while often uncomprehending and destructive, have also spurred Jews into more thoughtful or humane interpretations of their tradition. We Jews are for instance offended when non-Jews accuse us of being parochial, but the accusation in some ways hits home, and we have developed more universalistic practices in response to these criticisms. The criticisms Jews and Christians today make of violent or illiberal forms of Islam, while also often uncomprehending and destructive, may have a similar effect. And for hundreds of years, debates between Hindus and Buddhists in South Asia, and Confucians and Buddhists in China, shaped the self-understanding of each of these traditions. In our individual lives, we are acutely aware that the fear of looking silly or selfish or cruel in front of a stranger can lead us to make extra efforts to appear—and *be*—smart, unselfish, and humane. The presence of outsiders to our traditions can, and at its best does, have a similar impact on each religious community. Spiritual competition can be helpful to every participant in that competition: as long as the competition remains a spiritual one, and does not degenerate into insult and humiliation, or violence.

And if spiritual competition is valuable in this way, then it makes sense for those who think that the universe is governed by a good force or being to understand the plurality of religions as flowing from the will of that force or being, and for even non-theistic religions to regard their sparring partners as helping them refine and promote their vision for humanity. It makes sense, that is, for members of each religious tradition to regard the existence of other such traditions as a good thing, and to regard every other tradition as good as long as it too welcomes this diversity. We have no reason to respect religious communities who kill those who disagree with them, or try to frighten or manipulate people into joining their faith. These are not communities from whom we can learn in free and open debate; they are, instead, destructive of debate. (They are also immoral enough to give us reason to doubt that they have an adequate vision of the good for all humanity.) But we have every reason to respect communities that themselves honor the parameters of free and open debate: every reason to suppose that we may learn something from them. To every *such* community, the rabbinic adage I cited above can be adapted: "Despise no community, for each one has its hour."

Some might take these points to suggest that eventually all religions will converge into one. But that need not follow: religious traditions can remain distinct forever while still learning from one another. Others may accept these points while still believing that eventually everyone will accept their particular tradition. But even if we do all eventually join one religious tradition, that tradition may be altered by its interaction with other traditions. A certain degree of respect for other religions can thus be valued even by monists. A Christian or Muslim who thinks that eventually everyone should become Christian or Muslim can yet look forward to having Christianity and Islam improved by what it learns from other traditions. In the end, what we most need from religious believers is respect for other religions, if their commitments are to be compatible with liberal moral values. And we can achieve that even without pluralism.

Respect for other religions can provide believers with a model for how to regard the non-religious. Religious believers can respect secular people both in the sense that they can see the latter as having moral virtues and in the sense that they can hope to learn from secular practices and attitudes, including the very criticisms of religion that secularists make. That is not to say that religious believers can regard secular ways of life as just as good as their own. There is no getting around the fact that a religious believer, by dint of his or her religious commitments, implicitly rejects the telic views of secular people. To say that we cannot adequately find meaning or purpose in our lives by way of our natural faculties alone is to say that secular people, if honest with themselves, should see life as meaningless. That is not quite the same as saying that the lives of secular people *are* meaningless. A person may be wrong in how she views the human end while still achieving it. And some religious visions allow for a life that is not explicitly religious nevertheless to achieve God's will, be aligned with the *tao*, etc. A person who dedicates her life to struggling for the poor or oppressed is implicitly imitating Christ, one might say, or participating in holiness. Or one might see such religious ends carried out in a life dedicated to art or philosophy or care for family. Still, religious people are committed to the idea that only their religious visions properly explain *why* these activities are worthwhile. One can't very well give up this idea without giving up one's religion.

The idea is, however, offensive to many secular people. They are irritated by the suggestion that religious people have a grasp on what makes life worth living that they lack. Their offense is understandable but the proper response to it is a gentle reminder that secular people are just as committed to a rejection of the telic views held by religious people. They would not be secular unless they rejected beliefs in God, an afterlife, and the like. Even if they are polite enough not to express their views on these subjects to religious people, they must in the end regard the latter as mistaken. Often, of course, secular people are not so polite: people who declare that belief in God is superstitious and childish are hardly in short supply. But others think that they show respect for religious believers by saying that they understand, and want to support, our desire to live religiously—that our practices, because they matter to us, are every bit as valuable as their own concern for art or baseball or whatever. They value our religious practices as they value other lifestyles, and they believe that all people ought to be able to pursue the style of life they care about, as long as they don't hurt others. But they are mistaken if they think this is really respect for religious commitment. For those of us who are religious do not see ourselves as pursuing just one "life-style" among others, and do not pursue it just because it engages our desires, as others might pursue art or baseball. We pursue it because we think it represents the highest good for all humanity. Indeed, it can and often does *trump* what we happen to desire, and call on us to renounce or modify what we would most enjoy doing. Secularists of the sort I've been describing—who try to be open to religion by seeing it as a life-style—should realize that they are implicitly endorsing an alternative view of the human highest good, by which it consists in pursuing any morally decent way of life that human beings happen to choose. At the end of the day, this is a view in conflict with religious views of the highest good, and secularists endorse it precisely insofar as they trace the worth of life to human choice, and reject the idea that that worth might instead need to be revealed by a supernatural source.

In short, religious and secular people need to accept that the differences between them amount to a disagreement over the nature of the highest good; mutual respect between them cannot depend on resolving or dissolving that disagreement. This should be unproblematic, as long as both groups can find reasons, despite their disagreement, to value something about how the other lives, and to hold out the possibility that they can learn from one another. And both groups can, I think, do that— exactly as people committed to one religion can find reason to respect people of other religions.

In the first place, religious and secular people of integrity and decency can endorse one another's moral virtues. Morality, once again, rests largely on modes of insight and argument that are independent of religion (it must do that, if it is to hold together societies made up of people with varying religious commitments), so it provides norms and ideals that religious and non-religious people can share. What religion adds to morality is a *frame* that puts moral norms and ideals in a new light—not, except in marginal cases, new content for those norms and ideals. A religion that proclaims murder, torture, or rape to be good, or helping those who suffer to be bad, simply convicts itself of not really being a religion at all: not really having a vision of the highest human good. Of course, on occasion there is interaction between our religious and our moral views. Especially when moral questions turn to a significant degree on telic ones—when we are trying to determine the true beginning or end of human life, for instance, which is hard to do without a conception of what gives human life value—equally thoughtful and decent people may disagree sharply over their resolution. And religious traditions draw heavily on their telic visions for the norms they propose for resolving these debates. But there will be little difference between the approach of a religious and a secular person to most moral issues.

So religious and secular people can work together on many moral projects. It is just that the religious person will have somewhat different reasons for her moral commitments than will a secular person. A religious Christian or Jew who participates in a struggle for immigrant rights may work alongside secular people committed to the same cause, may do exactly what they do, and may give many of the same reasons for her actions: that the people she is trying to help deserve freedom and dignity, that their suffering warrants compassion, or that oppressing or ignoring these people de-humanizes us. But she may add that her ultimate aim is not to see her fellow human beings *merely* politically free and materially happy. Rather, she hopes they will be able to use their improved political and material condition as a means to achieve the ultimate human good. Or she sees the struggle for human rights as part of her own religious path. Perhaps she regards the bringing of other human beings out of suffering and oppression as a means to Buddhist enlightenment, for the oppressor as well as the victim. Or she may see ending suffering and oppression as an expression of her love for God, and for the image of God in other people. In any of these and many other ways the religious person can have reason to take moral duties as themselves religious duties, and to respect secular people who carry out those same duties. The religious and the secular person both believe, after all, in the importance of freedom, well-being, and human dignity. They simply have different conceptions of how those goods fit into the overall human good.

But even in the telic realm, there is much that a religious and a secular person will share. After all, human beings come to whatever view they hold of the highest good for humanity from the same questions and intuitions. We share the questions leading us to seek an overall human good, and we share many intuitions about what sorts of activities should figure in a plausible account of that good. This provides a direct and an indirect way for secular and religious people to learn from one another.

The fact that we share telic intuitions directly entails that we can learn from one another. The Aristotelian, the Marxist, and the devout Christian will all agree that raising children is a great human good, even while the Aristotelian sees this good as properly directed towards educating the next generation in virtue, the Marxist sees it as properly directed toward building a classless society, and the Christian thinks that ideally it should lead one's children to Jesus. These are sharp disagreements, but they arise out of an agreed starting point, and even when they are not resolved, the Aristotelian, Marxist, and Christian can teach one another aspects of good child-raising. Many of us who are not Marxists have nevertheless learned from them about the importance of egalitarian procedures within the family, and many who are not Christians have nevertheless learned from Christian family worship about the value of sharing one's ideals with one's children. This is not to deny that we sometimes see the telic views of others as getting in the way of their appreciation of more limited goods: Marxists who approve only of art that furthers the class struggle, and religious people who regard sentimental pictures of their saints as high art, rarely win over others to their views on this subject. But we also can and do learn more about particular goods across wide differences over the ultimate or overall good.

The fact that we share the questions leading us to seek an ultimate or overall human good makes for a more indirect sort of learning across telic differences. We all fear death and ennui; we all wonder how to prioritize our interests and commitments; we all seek pleasure but can be brought to doubt its value; and we all find apparent worth in art, erotic love, and intellectual achievement but can be brought to wonder whether these things are enough to make our lives worthwhile. Some people conclude that our pleasures or experience of art, eros, intellectual activity etc. *do* suffice to make our lives worth living, or that the question about the worth of life is irresolvable or incoherent and we should set it aside and throw ourselves into pleasure instead. These are people who return a secular response to the search for a highest human end, and one might think that their dismissal of that search, or satisfaction with a naturalistic answer to it, will close off conversation between them and religious people on the subject. But even people who dismiss the question about life's worth have usually at some point appreciated its force, and for that reason the claim of a religious person that she has been able to find value in her life only by way of a religious vision is likely to get some grip on them: to irritate them, if nothing else. This point works in the opposite direction as well. Many religious people have wondered whether living for pleasure, or for the fulfillment of their natural capacities, might be enough to make their lives worthwhile—have wondered whether their religious beliefs are silly, and a distraction from living for the only goods human beings are capable of achieving. They, in turn, normally find something gripping, therefore, about a secular approach to the telic question: are, at least, irritated by it.

And this grip, even irritation, is an opening for conversation. Secular people often find the critique of naturalistic telic views powerful. The idea that living for pleasure, or for art and eros, etc. is vanity, idolatry, or a path to endless suffering strikes many secular people as plausible, even if they don't in the end accept it. On the other hand, religious people generally think that they need to show how their path can accommodate the goodness of pleasure, art, eros, intellectual achievement, and the like. Secular and religious people thus do not simply talk past one another on telic questions, and they can sharpen their answers to those questions by talking with one another. Of course, they differ deeply over whether it is reasonable to suppose that our ultimate good is essentially obscure, to trust a text that purports to reveal that obscure good to us, or to put faith in the metaphysical presuppositions that this trust brings with it. And they cannot overcome these differences unless one side gives up its secularity or the other its religiousness. But there remains much they can learn from one another about particular goods and about what an account of the overall human good should look like. That is enough for mutual respect.

Finally, people of all religions and none should realize that they gain from a public sphere that encourages the pursuit of a wide variety of telic views, and is dominated by none. Elsewhere I have called this an enlightened public sphere, and it is close to what John Rawls calls a society governed by public reason, and Jürgen Habermas describes as a public realm that approximates the ideal speech situation. From the perspective of each religion, the others appear as at best partial or clouded versions of the true or ideal human path. From the perspective of each secular telic view, other secular telic views, and all religions, appear as at best partial or clouded versions of the true or ideal human path. Only a public sphere that is neutral among these alternatives, and allows as many of them as possible to express themselves, can afford us the opportunity to change our mind about them: converting from one religion to another, or abandoning religion, or moving from a secular way of life to a religious one. Holding open these possibilities also allows us to be confident, when we stick with the view we already have, that we are doing so freely, rather than out of social or political pressure. Having access to a public square filled with alternative ways of life, and open debate over them, also allows each of us to make clear to ourselves the reasons why we hold whatever view we do. And it gives us a space in which we can voice criticisms of our religious leaders—for corruption or oppressiveness, for being too rigid, or for not being strict or devout enough—or to break away from the group to which we belong and join a dissenting sub-group.

That would not be possible if our own group dominated the public sphere. A public sphere dominated by advocates of another religion, or by advocates of a secular view of the human good, would also of course be oppressive to us. Only an open public space filled with representatives of many telic views, secular and religious, provides us all with a neutral zone through which we can move whenever we feel the need to assess the visions we have been pursuing—a breathing space, as it were, free of the pressures we experience in the midst of our telic communities. This breathing space will lead some people to drop their commitments or alter them, while others will just consider doing that, and return to their community with renewed fervor. But the fact that we *can* drop our commitments or alter them should reassure us that the commitments we have, even when we maintain them intact, are freely chosen.

An open public space, filled with a diversity of religious and secular voices, thus guarantees the freedom of our religious beliefs: it enables them to be truly *ours*, rather than a product of fear or ignorance. And the value of this freedom provides all of us—secular and religious alike—to see a real good in the fact that the others are there to hold up alternative worldviews. As long as each group sees that, and remains committed to free and open debate across such views, we can achieve a deep and robust respect for one another.

So belief in revealed religion of the sort I have been urging can go along with a strong commitment to mutual respect among religions, and between religious and secular people. The fact that revelation, on my account, does not operate by way of reason alone is important to this respect. The obscurity of our views, and their dependence on affective conditions as well as argument, should keep believers from seeing their view as clearly correct. It would be helpful if secular people also recognized that questions about our highest good are extremely difficult, and answers to them may be essentially obscure, or at least fall short of persuading every reasonable person. Accepting this much of the religious person's attitude toward life would encourage a welcome humility on the part of secularists that is often missing today. At any rate, a secular person who honestly wants to respect religious people, and not merely to tolerate them, would do well to keep him or herself open to the possibility that a cryptic vision of the good, rooted in a non-naturalistic metaphysics, could just possibly be correct. Science and morality do not rule out such a possibility, after all. And only if we all remain open to it can we expect fruitful telic discussions between religious and secular people. Only then can religious and secular people expect to learn much from one another on telic matters; only then can they proceed together in the search for an ultimate or overall human good.

Conclusion

I have described a way that people *can* follow a revealed religion—aware of the non-rational sources of their commitments and consequently open, flexible, and respectful of other religions and of secular people—not the way that most people *do* follow such religions. We read every day about religious people killing each other, depriving others of rights, and perpetrating all manner of other murder and mayhem. We also read about religious people who set themselves up in opposition to modern science, on everything from evolution to the health implications of abortion. And when we read about religious people with admirable moral virtues, or a thoughtful approach to science, they tend to have a rationalist conception of religion, only loosely tied to a revealed text and a tradition of receiving that text.

But more traditional religious commitments, rooted in the idea that certain texts and teachings come from God, can also go together with liberal virtues and an affirmation of modern science. If a traditional text or teaching has something to offer to every age, as it must if its author is God, then it should fit the modern world as well as the ancient or medieval one. Moreover, those of us who believe in God should see God's hand behind the moral and cognitive achievements of modernity. To come to revelation after first affirming the truth of a naturalistic science and the decency of a naturalistic morality also enables us to see, more sharply, the distinctively *non*-naturalistic cast of this means of telic guidance. We understand more deeply how much we are casting off our ordinary, naturalistic way of getting around the world in opting for a revealed religion—how much we are taking a "leap of faith"—if we appreciate first the good things that that ordinary, naturalistic worldliness can accomplish.

So revelation need not replace secularized reason. It can and should graft itself, instead, onto our ordinary, secular ways of thinking and acting. Abraham is often cited as an example of someone who suspends all ordinary moral and pragmatic concerns when he offers up his beloved son to a supernatural God. But that same Abraham is figured in the Bible, earlier, as challenging God Himself to live up to an independent standard of justice: "Shall not the Judge of all the earth do justly?" (Genesis 18:25). That same Abraham can also be read as breaking off a conversation with God in order to take care of what he thinks are three human guests (Genesis 18:1–2). These aspects of Abraham provide a better model for religious commitment than the aspect by which he unquestioningly offers up his son. We build first a just and decent community with our fellow human beings, independently of revelation and religious belief. Only then does God appear to us.

That doesn't mean that our secular ways of thinking are adequate in themselves. But what is missing in them, what they cannot accomplish, becomes clear only when we give them free rein to demonstrate what they can accomplish. God's Word is uncanny, sublime, radically different from what we ordinarily think and say, and it displays its sublimity only when we allow it to set itself against our ordinary way of being.

In any case, a thoughtful and decent religious life consists in combining secular ways of seeking truth and moral goodness with a commitment to a revealed text and path. We might call someone who exemplifies this combination a worldly saint. The gentle rabbi Hillel, combining unwavering devotion with a dry sense of humor; Thomas Aquinas, integrating Christian doctrine with the best science of his day; the current Dalai Lama, representing his community politically in difficult times, while exemplifying the best of Buddhist thought and practice—all these are examples of the worldly saint. But it is simplest to stick with Abraham. For Abraham is *both* the other-worldly devotee who is willing to give all to God *and* the worldly fellow who travels to a strange land, builds a great clan, interacts with kings and merchants on terms independent of his religious commitments, and—except for the one shocking moment where he offers up his son—takes care of other human beings as well as, even before, attending to God. Indeed, Kierkegaard, who focuses on the shocking moment, also gives us an astute and witty portrait of the more complex believer that Abraham generally represents:

Here [is the knight of faith].... The moment I set eyes on him I instantly push him from me, I myself leap backwards, I clasp my hands and say half aloud,

"Good Lord, is this the man? Is it really he? Why, he looks like a tax-collector!" However, it is the man after all. I draw closer to him, watching his least movements to see whether there might not be visible a little heterogeneous fractional telegraphic message from the infinite, a glance, a look, a gesture, a note of sadness, a smile, which betrayed the infinite in its heterogeneity with the finite. No! I examine his figure from tip to toe to see if there might not be a cranny through which the infinite was peeping. No! He is solid through and through. His tread? It is vigorous, belonging entirely to finiteness; no smartly dressed towns-man who walks out to Fresberg on a Sunday afternoon treads the ground more firmly, he belongs entirely to the world, no Philistine more so. . . . [W]henever one sees him taking part in a particular pleasure, he does it with the persistence which is the mark of the earthly man whose soul is absorbed in such things. . . . He takes delight in everything he sees, in the human swarm, in the new omni-buses, in the water of the sound . . . Toward evening he walks home, his gait is as indefatigable as that of the postman. On his way he reflects that his wife has surely a special little warm dish prepared for him, e.g., a calf's head roasted, garnished with vegetables. If he were to meet a man like-minded, he could continue as far as East Gate to discourse with him about that dish, with a passion befitting a hotel chef. As it happens, he hasn't four pence to his name, and yet he fully and firmly believes that his wife has that dainty dish for him. If she had it, it would then be an invidious sight for superior people and an inspiring one for the plain man to see him eat; for his appetite is greater than Esau's. His wife hasn't it—strangely enough, it is quite the same to him. On the way he comes past a building site and runs across another man. They talk together for a moment. In the twinkling of an eye he erects a new building, he has at his disposition all the powers necessary for it. The stranger leaves him with the thought that he certainly was a capitalist, while my admired knight thinks, "Yes, if the money were needed, I dare say I could get it." . . . He lives as carefree as a ne'er-do-well, and yet he buys up the acceptable time at the dearest price, for he does not do the least thing except by virtue of the absurd. . . . [T]his man has made and every instant is making the movements of infinity. With infinite resignation he has drained the cup of life's profound sadness, he knows the bliss of the infinite, he senses the pain of renouncing everything, the dearest things he possesses in the world, and yet finiteness tastes to him just as good as to one who never knew anything higher . . . [T]he whole earthly form he exhibits is a new creation by virtue of the absurd. He resigned everything infinitely, and then he grasped everything again by virtue of the absurd. He constantly makes the movements of infinity, but he does this with such correctness and assurance that he gets the finite out of it.

On this picture, a worldly saint is a person who realizes how crazy it is, how utterly improbable, for there to be a God at the root of our petty and arbitrary world, in which we live from disappointment to disappoint-ment most of the time, yet who believes in that God anyway and, full of delight, sees His presence constantly in the very limitations that frustrate most of us. But to do this is to hold together our ordinary way of getting around the world—with its skeptical modes of inquiry, its dependence on the wheel of biological needs that drive most of what we do, and its hard moral demand that we respect all our not-so-pleasant fellow inquirers and need-satisfiers—with the hope or conviction that we stand in the presence of an ideally good, transforming Being, who gives all this drudgery a joyous significance. This faith shows most fully in a person who embraces our world like the sanest of folk at the same time that he stands beyond it: in the Abraham who builds a clan and negotiates water rights even while worshipping a transcendent God, who talks to God but suspends the conversation to get bread and meat for some travelers. For religious as well as secular reasons, we need to render unto Caesar what is Caesar's and unto God what is God's. We need to give the way of the ordinary human world its rightful respect, while still recognizing that it stands in need of revelation, and gains its true significance by giving revelation a home. The knight of faith enjoys his meat and his new buildings, but it is part of his faith to understand that faith itself does not make meat or buildings; the human community, religious and secular alike, does that.

Pace Kierkegaard himself, this means that a worldly saint cannot give up his moral commitments in the way he can give up his hopes. His moral commitments belong to the human community, not to him: they are not his to give up. So, no, he cannot kill his beloved son. Abraham's willingness to sacrifice Isaac has always been a terrifying mystery to believers. It remains that; we are and should be disturbed by it, not hold it up as a model of faith, as Kierkegaard does. That said, in the passage I have quoted Kierkegaard gives us a wonderful description of the worldly saint, of how religious commitment and secular ways of getting around the world can fit together. The worldly saint seems first of all and most of the time indistinguishable from a wholly secular person. But his union with this finite world of ours comes about, as the secular person's does not, only because he constantly makes the movements of infinity: his rationality comes about only by virtue of the absurd.

Notes

1 *Deuteronomy 24:5*: See note on translations from the Hebrew Bible under "Bible" in the Bibliography.

4 ... *rather than ... by way of personal experience or intuition* ... I thus want to defend, not New Age religions, nor progressive forms of Christianity and Judaism that appeal to moral or mystical experiences, but the traditional religions that these groups seek to replace.

4 *Kant already complained* ... "A holy book commands the greatest respect even among those (indeed, among these most of all) who do not read it, ... and no subtle argument can stand up to the knockdown pronouncement, *Thus it is written.*": Kant (1998), p. 116 (Ak 6:107).

6 *Chapter 1: Truth.* This chapter summarizes Part I of Fleischacker (2011).

6 *Revealed religion* ... This was a common phrase in the eighteenth century, generally contrasted with "natural religion." "Natural religion" referred to a trimmed-down set of religious beliefs that were thought to be built into human nature and rationally defensible: in God, in the centrality of virtue to the worship of God, and in an afterlife, in which our virtue will be rewarded. "Revealed religion"—also called "positive" or "historical" religion—adds to these beliefs the doctrines that distinguish Christianity, Islam, Buddhism, etc. from one another: the giving of law on Sinai, the Incarnation and Resurrection, or the idea that Muhammed is God's last and greatest prophet. In general, eighteenth-century defenders of religion favored natural over revealed religion; others defended revealed religion by saying that it amounted to a colorful way of expressing natural religion. I am concerned here to defend revealed religion *rather than* natural religion—and not by reducing revelation to a colorful way of expressing rational principles.

10 ... *predictive and technological payoff* ... These are generally taken to be marks of successful factual explanation by all human beings: see Taylor (1984).

10 ... *"new religious rationalists"* ... The main figures I have in mind under this heading are Alvin Plantinga, William Alston, Nicholas Wolterstorff, and Richard Swinburne. Representative writings include Alston (1993), Plantinga (2000), and Swinburne (2004). I use the name "new religious rationalists" for them to suggest that they resemble medieval rationalists like ibn Sina,

Maimonides, and Aquinas, who thought that religion could be readily reconciled with science. That makes better sense in the context of medieval science, which worked with a conception of nature that requires a God, than it does today. Fideism—views, like Kierkegaard's, on which a non-rational faith is crucial to religious commitment—are, I think, better suited to the modern world. For further discussion, see Fleischacker (2011), Part I, Chapter 1 and Part IV, Chapter 1.

12 *In several of his books*... See Plantinga (1993), Chapter 12; Plantinga (2000), pp. 227–40; and Plantinga (2011), Chapter 10.

12 *Plantinga says that*... Plantinga (2000), pp. 234–5.

13 *We will do best to treat Plantinga's argument... as a supplement*... And a constraint on what that God must be like: it should be a God Who wants us to achieve knowledge of our universe. That gives us religious reasons to respect science, and to abjure silly attacks on it.

14 *Some Christian writers*... Richard Swinburne has made this claim repeatedly. See for instance Swinburne (1992), Chapter 6.

14 *Moses Mendelssohn*... Mendelssohn (1983), p. 87.

15 *... even if we met Jesus... and followed him around day and night*... Compare Kierkegaard (1962), Chapter IV.

16 *Maimonides says*... Maimonides (1962), Part II, Chapter 25.

17 *Genesis 24:48–49*: See note on translations from the Hebrew Bible under "Bible" in the Bibliography.

18 *It calls on us instead to trust it*... One reader for this book suggested that moving from truth as accuracy to truth as trustworthiness doesn't help much, as regards the Bible. Why should we trust the Bible, he asked, when scholars agree that it was (in his words) "a falsification of history [written] by.... priests ... to justify their seizure of political power"?

Well, in the first place, this is an outdated conception of what Biblical scholars agree on. Few would now attribute the Bible's authorship solely to priests. Few would regard the Bible's authors as deliberately falsifying history—they are seen, rather, as largely passing down legends whose origins they themselves did not know, and treating their sources with great reverence. And few would reduce their motives to anything as simplistic as a "seizure of political power." The reaction of this reader reflects the attitudes—often anti-Semitic, always anti-clerical, and generally informed by a crudely egoistic conception of human nature—of early Biblical scholarship in the nineteenth century. Far more nuanced accounts are prevalent today, which allow that the human authors of the Bible were doing their best to express the truth about God and Israelite history as they understood it.

But even if the early, harsher view were correct, and the authors of the Hebrew Bible were out for power alone, that would not entail that what they wrote must be ethically or religiously untrustworthy. For the believer in a religious scripture takes *God*, not the human beings who wrote its components, to be its ultimate source, and it is God, not those human beings, in which she puts her trust. God, however, might work through scoundrels. The Bible indeed suggests as much, in the story of Balaam. The stories of Saul's prophesy and of Jonah also indicate that God can work through very flawed vessels. And surely God could lay out a path for us by way of legends and commands whose human authors intended them for different purposes. In any case, as we'll see later, the reasons for trusting a scripture should be drawn solely from the ethical plausibility of its content. How that content was produced is irrelevant.

23 *. . . shift from a literal to a metaphorical register . . .* I discuss this sort of shift in detail in Fleischacker (1994) and Fleischacker (2011), Part I, Chapter IV and Part IV, Chapter 6.

24 *. . . says one rabbi . . .* Quoted from the Zohar (III:152a) in Scholem (1965), p. 64. I return to this text in Chapter 6, page 104.

26 *Chapter 2: Ethics.* This chapter summarizes Part II of Fleischacker (2011).

27 *. . . reflect this tension . . .* The two-sidedness of the good will also figure in my account of interpretation in Chapter 6: we rely on our independent understanding of goodness to interpret revelation, even as we recognize that we need revelation to grasp our full or overall good.

31 *Plato noted . . .* In the *Euthyphro* 7b–d. See Plato (1997), pp. 6–7.

32 *. . . must account for both our agreement and our disagreement . . .* A set of profound meditations on this theme can be found in Cavell (1979), Part III.

34 *I propose from now on . . .* A similar distinction is drawn in Williams (1985), p. 6, Habermas (1995), pp. 98–101 and 178, and Donagan (1999), pp. 191–4.

36 *. . . Ashoka, included a similar principle . . .* See Rahula (1974), pp. 4–5, 87–8.

36 *. . . Thomas Aquinas . . . declared . . .* See Aquinas (1953), p. 68 (Summa Theologica I-II Q 96, A2).

37 *Some have proposed . . .* See Scanlon (1998) and Gaus (2012).

38 *They may cite Scriptural verses . . .* But in fact there are few verses in either the Jewish or the Christian Bible that say anything about abortion. One (Exodus 21:22) seems to *deny* that a fetus is a full human being.

38 *For religious arguments to be moral arguments . . .* As we'll see shortly, abortion and other end-of-life issues do however raise telic questions, which gives religion a bearing on them.

45 *Chapter 3: Our Overall Good.* This chapter summarizes Part III of Fleischacker (2011).

45 *Our practice refutes our doubts...* "My practice, you say, refutes my doubts," writes Hume in his *Enquiry Concerning Human Understanding* (1975; Section IV, Part II), in the voice of an objector to his scepticism about causality. Hume goes on, here, to push off this pragmatic response to scepticism, but elsewhere he embraces it. I think pragmatism often offers a good response to scepticism. But when it comes to doubts about life's meaning, as we'll see momentarily, we have *pragmatic* reasons for taking those doubts seriously.

50 *...a wonderful* Peanuts *strip...* A reader for this book noted that the moral philosopher Peter Singer has addressed the *Peanuts* problem. In an engaging book entitled *How are We to Live?* (Singer 1995), Singer argues that the best way to find meaning in life is to commit oneself to ethical projects. He even declares that "no amount of reflection will show a commitment to an ethical life to be trivial or pointless" (p. 218). And he reports from his own experience that the people he knows who are committed to lessening the suffering in the world are "not bored and do not need psychotherapy to make their lives meaningful" (p. 222). Then he says:

> There is a tragic irony in the fact that we can find our own fulfillment precisely because there is so much avoidable pain and suffering in the universe, but that is the way the world is. The task will not be completed until we can no longer find children stunted from malnutrition or dying from easily treatable infections; homeless people trying to keep warm with pieces of cardboard; political prisoners held without trial; [etc.] ... How we would find meaning in our lives if all avoidable pain and suffering had been eliminated is an interesting topic for philosophical discussion, but the question is, sadly, unlikely to have any practical significance for the foreseeable future. (pp. 222–3).

It is worth noting that Singer doesn't clearly say here that a life in which no one had to struggle against avoidable pain and suffering would *necessarily* be without meaning, but he certainly leaves that open as a possibility. If that were the case, however, Singer's picture of meaning would be a very strange one. We, the people who suffer and struggle today, find meaning in our lives by trying to bring about a world in which other people will have meaning*less* lives. Transfer the scenario to an individual life and it becomes obviously absurd. It may *seem* as if I am doing something terribly important when I try to remove the avoidable pain and suffering from my life, but that appearance will be shown up as hollow if I succeed and then find nothing important about what I do. If my life seemed meaningful only when I was struggling to overcome pain, then if I do overcome it I will regard the appearance of meaning in my efforts to do so as *merely* an appearance: an illusion that arose from an otherwise bad condition. But if this is true in my own case, it is true globally too: removing the pain from other people's lives will simply expose the appearance of "meaning" or "fulfillment," in our efforts to remove that pain, to be illusory. How can removing pain from people's lives matter unless the lives from which it is removed matter?—but then they must matter independently of having the pain removed.

I suspect that Singer actually believes that the impression that removing pain and suffering gives meaning to our lives *is* an illusion: but a useful one, since it helps get us to do what morality demands of us. Singer is a utilitarian, and it is in line with long-standing utilitarian theses to encourage us to hold on to illusions so long as they are morally useful. But in that case, what he says in the passage above is disingenuous. Life is *not* made "fulfilling" or given "meaning" by our helping others—we simply *should* do that, and can enjoy the *illusion* that our lives are meaningful if we do. For utilitarians, either life is fulfilling just by being pleasurable or it is a mistake to try to think of it in terms of fulfillment—the concept of fulfillment or worth or meaning gets no purchase, once we distinguish it from pleasure.

51 ... *is of course erotic love* ... The love of friends may be deeper and more lasting than erotic love, but is unlikely to strike anyone as the end to which our whole lives are devoted. We understand it better, I think, as something that *accompanies* whatever that end might be (this is how Aristotle understood virtuous friendship). We want to share whatever we take to be ultimately valuable with friends, but friendship itself is not sufficient to constitute that end.

55 ... *then any value we see in* all *the spheres* ... This would not be the case if what was wrong with our sense that each sphere is valuable depended on our failure to connect that value with the value of the other spheres. But the interconnectedness of spheres played no role in the debunking arguments I have offered.

56 *From ancient times* ... Ecclesiastes, for instance, periodically uses the claim that all is vanity, and life is pointless, as a basis for saying that we should eat, drink, and enjoy ourselves (5:17, 8:15, 9:7–9).

57 *As Aristotle put it* ... Aristotle (1984), Vol. 2, p. 1860 (Nicomachean Ethics: 1176b29–30).

58 *Jonathan Haidt* ... *suggests* ... Haidt (2006), pp. 238–9.

59 *"Why should I live?* ... " Tolstoy (1983), pp. 34–5. See also pp. 36–42.

62 *A good that is* difficult *to know*...Compare the discussion of "dialectical activity" in Brewer (2009).

63 *A number of Christian theologians*...See especially Kierkegaard (1962). On paradox in the Madhyamaka school of Buddhism, see Garfield (1995), p. 102.

65 *It is not in science or morality but in our search for an adequate telos*... "[T]heology is relevant to ethics not principally with regard to morality, but with regard to the question of what life is for.": Donagan (1999), p. 194, emphasis removed. Donagan also denies that religions offer us anything much of scientific value (p. 12).

66 *Chapter 4: Revelation.* This chapter summarizes Fleischacker (2011), Part IV, Chapters 2–5.

66 *"I placed a jar in Tennessee"*...Stevens (2011).

67 ...*as defenders of religion sometimes think*...Robert Gordis and Abraham Joshua Heschel both drew a sharp contrast between the "inspiration" of artists and the "revelation" of prophets. The *Niagara Bible Conference Creed*, a statement of principles by conservative Christian biblical scholars, drew a similar distinction while using the word "inspiration" for both groups: see Fleischacker (2011), p. 527, n. 45 and text thereto.

70 *But we also saw in Chapter 1*...See pp. 13 and 25.

71 ...*bards who pass on certain stories as sacred*...See Finley (1979), pp. 39–42

71 ...*internal dialogue we carry out with ourselves*...Hannah Arendt liked to describe thinking as "the soundless dialogue between me and myself." See especially Arendt (1978), Vol. I ("Thinking"), pp. 184–93.

72 ...*"spiritual but not religious"*...See Oppenheimer (2014).

72 *"Religion" in its origin means "to be bound"*...At least that is one common and plausible etymology of the word. Hannah Arendt employs this etymology to fruitful effect in her "What is Authority?": see Arendt (1968), p. 121.

76 *Consider Eknath Easwaran's account*...Easwaran, (1987), p. 8

77 *"I sneered"*...Meta (1993), pp. 31–2

78 ...*calls such restraint "holiness"*...This is the standard Jewish understanding of holiness. For a deep and beautiful expression of it, see Nachmanides' commentary on Leviticus 19:2 (Nachmanides 1974), Vol. III, pp. 282–4.

78 ...*I see myself as standing, each day, at Sinai*...As I understand Maimonides' 8th principle of faith, it calls on us to see ourselves as constantly at Sinai: see Fleischacker (2014). The same idea can be found in the Zohar: "Every day he who is worthy receives the Torah standing at Sinai; he hears the Torah from the mouth of the Lord.": Vol. I, p. 90a, as quoted in Heschel (1955), p. 146.

79 . . . *beautifies morality and moralizes beauty* . . . How are the moral and the beautiful aspects of revelation supposed to interact?, well, perhaps developing a moral character, in addition to helping others, helps me to restrain my excessive passions and desires so that I can properly see the beauty in, or opened up by, a revealed text. Aristotle thought that virtue could be a condition for certain sorts of perception, including the perception of what is valuable in contemplation—our highest good, for him. An analogous thought runs through the Buddhist tradition: only the virtuous person has the emotional capacity to grasp the truths that end suffering.

Alternatively, perhaps the beautiful vision that satisfies our telic yearnings is meant to go out to human beings in community, and virtue is a condition for building communities that can accept such a revelation. Perhaps God wants us to help each other reach a position in which we are free enough of oppression and material want that we can turn our attention to telic questions. Or perhaps God withholds the vision of our full good until we first recognize, and honor, the image of divinity in each other.

Yet another possibility is that the beauty of a telic vision keeps us committed to morality. Perhaps moral evil springs above all from the fear that our lives are pointless, and an answer to our telic worries is therefore an answer to our moral problems as well. It is not implausible that many people indulge in violence and cruelty, greed and betrayal, out of a fear of boredom and death. A vision that inspires them with a sense of the intrinsic value of their lives, or that is itself endlessly fascinating, may then take them out of the psychological conditions leading them to evil. The beauty of revelation would thus help solve moral problems—revelation would make morality interesting, exciting, moving, in a way that it is not when we see it as merely enabling society to survive, maximizing happiness, and the like.

81 *Christianity . . . [has] a more individualist tendency* . . . Jesus' polemic against relying too much on one's family—see Matthew 8:21–22, 10:37, or 12:46–50—may play into this tendency.

82 . . . *sometimes run by Orthodox Jews* . . . The best example I know of an Orthodox human rights organization is *Uri l'Tzedek*, in New York. But Orthodox Jews work together with Reform and Conservative Jews to support Rabbis for Human Rights, the Association for Civil Rights in Israel, and other organizations.

83 *Chapter 5: Ethical Faith.* This chapter covers issues discussed more fully in Fleischacker (2011), Part II, Chapter 5, §§ 40–49 and Part IV, Chapter 1.

83 . . . *find it hard to see* . . . One ancient Jewish teaching has it that this life is an antechamber to the life to come, and we should prepare ourselves here for the grand hall inside. I find this a helpful idea. It makes sense to me that a good

God might give us such brief and disappointing lives if what we are supposed to do with them is like the putting off of coats and wiping of shoes that goes on in an antechamber, and the full purpose of our existence will become clear when we stop having to care for our bodies and enter a spiritual realm. A grand hall inside would give the antechamber a purpose. But if there is no grand hall, the antechamber becomes ridiculous. What a bizarre exercise in futility our lives would be if they consisted just in an endless putting off of coats and wiping of shoes!

84   ... *a reasonable hope, Kant says* ... On this subject, see Chignell (forthcoming).

85   ... *Thomas Wizenmann asked Kant* ... See Kant (1956), p. 151n (Ak 5:143–4n). Wizenmann's charge, according to Frederick Beiser, was actually that a man might on Kant's principles use his love for a woman as a reason for thinking that she loves him: Beiser (1987), p. 120. But Kant construes the charge as I have described it.

86   ... *the same sorts of complaint today* ... One web commentator on a review of Fleischacker (2011) said that my argument for faith can equally justify belief in the Flying Spaghetti Monster: <http://www.newappsblog.com/2012/03/on-the-journeys-of-faith.html#comments>.

86   *To which Kant had several answers.* My reading of Kant here is based largely on the above-mentioned footnote—Kant (1956), p. 151n (Ak 5:143–4n)—but also on the "Dialectic" in the Second Critique more generally, along with elements of a number of Kant's other writings on religion. For sources, and a fuller argument for this reading, see Fleischacker (2011), pp. 150–7.

88   *In a remarkable section of the* Republic ... Republic 508d–509a. See Plato (1997), p. 1129.

88   *That rules out* ... Belief in the Easter bunny could however be radically reinterpreted so that it is not subject to scientific determination and does serve to underwrite a conception of the highest good. The Easter bunny, a devotee might say, is a vast, benevolent, and life-transforming power underlying the universe, presented only mythically as a bunny. But *this* Easter bunny looks a lot like God. The "bunny" persona falls away, and we have the sort of metaphysical entity that a traditional religion might presuppose. This is a plausible object of belief, on my view—but the belief is no longer in (what we ordinarily call) the Easter bunny. Only *as* a magical object that hops around on the Christian spring holiday is the Easter bunny a silly object of belief: and the objection to Kantian faith from the Easter bunny must maintain it in this easily-dismissed form.

89   ... *world-picture* ... *judgment* ... For the notion of world-pictures, and the importance of judgment to their grounding, see Wittgenstein (1977). Much

of what I said about judgment in Fleischacker (1999) was inspired by Wittgenstein's *On Certainty*.

91 *But we do not, cannot, love reason alone* . . . Pace Plato (on some readings), Kant, and such Platonists and Kantians as Hermann Cohen. Cohen is reputed to have said, when asked how one can love an idea, "how can one love anything *but* an idea?" Although I can think of defenses for this claim (don't we love the ideas our spouses and parents stand for? don't we withdraw love even from them, if they betray our idea of humanity?), the palpable absurdity of this extreme rationalism should be enough to lead us to a different picture of love.

92 *As we saw in the previous chapter* . . . See pp. 74–5. I elaborate the "guidance" metaphor for religious trust or faith in detail in Fleischacker (2011), Book IV, Chapter 1.

93 *Chapter 6: Receiving Revelation.* This chapter parallels Fleischacker (2011), Book IV, Chapter 6.

93 *According to one legend* . . . The two legends can be found at *Babylonian Talmud* (BT) Shabbat 88a and *Sifre Devarim* 343, respectively. In the first of these passages, one rabbi questions whether a covenant made under coercion can possibly be a covenant at all; the second version of the Sinai story may represent a response to this objection.

94 . . . *no contract can depend on a threat* . . . I am grateful to David Novak (private communication) for stressing the importance of this aspect of the passage to me.

94 . . . *so-called "fundamentalists"* . . . After a Protestant movement that insisted on a particularly literalist reading of Scriptures. The term is not well-suited to Jews, Muslims, Catholics, or Hindus.

95 . . . *homoerotic poetry in the Middle Ages* . . . See Boswell (1980), pp. 233–9, HaNagid (1996), pp. 15–19 and the notes by Peter Cole, translator of the HaNagid volume, in HaNagid (1996), pp. 167–8.

97 . . . *can be recognized as . . . good . . . by all humanity.* The tradition adhering to the revelation need not represent its vision as something that all human beings must *accept*; it needs simply to represent it as something they could recognize as a *plausible version* of their highest good.

What can it mean to say that a vision is a plausible version of the highest good for all humanity, if not that every human being should accept it? Here are a few possibilities:

(i) The vision is an example or model of the highest good for everyone. It is, say, one way of being ascetic and, to achieve our highest good, we all ought to be ascetic. Or it is intellectually challenging and to achieve our highest good, we all need to be intellectually challenged. Or it develops our love for all sentient beings, and we all need to develop such love.

(ii) The vision helps bring about a condition in which all human beings achieve their highest end but does not bring about that condition on its own. By promoting a strong commitment to justice or nonviolence, say, the group that embraces this vision helps the rest of humanity get closer to a world in which justice will reign everywhere, at which point God will show us how all our telic questions are properly answered.

(iii) The vision in fact leads all human beings to achieve their highest good but only some human beings need explicitly *recognize* that that is how they are reaching their end. On some Christian views, for instance, Christ's death and resurrection provides salvation to everyone whether they realize that or not. The works of grace by which Christ shows up in people's lives may then not be explicitly Christian ones. The worship of a devout Jew or Hindu may, for such Christians, be expressions of God's salvation even though the Jew or Hindu doesn't see what she is doing as having anything to do with Christ.

A revelation can thus be understood as just one way of imagining or realizing the highest good for all humanity, or as realizing only a part of that end. What it cannot do is maintain that its telos is the end just of an individual or a limited human group. We are led to revelation by questions about whether human beings *generally* have an end, and an answer to those questions must respond to us *as* human beings generally, not just as individuals or groups. So any revelation needs to hold that its vision and path is a way by which any human being can attain the highest good, and that those who follow this way will contribute to, rather than obstructing, the good of all other human beings. In this sense, all revealed visions must be universal. There is no need for them to be universal in the stronger sense that they hold out their vision as the sole correct representation of the highest good, or the sole way to achieve that good.

99   *... rabbinic tale ...* BT Shabbat 31a; I have slightly altered the translation to be found in Dorff (1996), pp. 74–5.

100   *... cries out for figurative interpretation ...* The famous medieval Jewish commentator known as Rashi declares that the very first verse of the Torah "says nothing except 'Interpret me figuratively!' *(darshani)*." But if that is what the opening verse does, it is reasonable to suppose that the rest of the book may similarly require figurative interpretation *(drash)*; in

opening His book this way, God is signaling to us that we should be prepared to employ *drash* throughout. I'll argue shortly that *drash* is indeed the key to a religious sensibility.

101 *What the rabbis of the Talmud do with this passage* . . . See BT Sanhedrin 68b–72a.

101 *. . . perhaps the very teaching* . . . There are other possible lessons. For further discussion, see Fleischacker (2011), Part IV, §§ 62–4.

103 *. . . bring the Torah into line* . . . On the "eye for an eye" passages, see BT Baba Kamma 83b–84a. On capital punishment, see Mishnah Makkoth 1:10 (BT Makkoth 7a). An implicit endorsement of the dignity of every individual is usually seen in the declaration that all human beings are formed in the image of God (Genesis 1:27).

It is worth noting that the features of rabbinic interpretation mentioned in this paragraph brought Jewish societies closer to what today we consider justice and mercy than many other pre-modern cultures. Roman law allowed parents the right to execute their children, and made frequent, careless use of capital punishment. Almost all Christian societies executed people with abandon until recent times, and the United States, one of the most strongly Christian nations in the modern world, continues to do so. Rights of women to divorce were not present in many societies, including, again, Christian ones, until quite recently, and in many places, women were either not asked at all, or asked only nominally, for their consent before entering into marriage. I don't mean to suggest that rabbinic Judaism overcame sexism—it was and remains sexist in many ways, and even the rights it established for women as regards marriage and divorce were inadequate. But it is remarkable how much the rabbinic world, often pilloried by Christians as the paradigm of a hidebound, bigoted culture, in fact recognized certain Enlightenment ideals long before the rest of the world came to them.

103 *The rabbis of the Talmud* . . . On marital rape, see BT Eruvin 100b. On women's right to a divorce, see the texts and discussion in Riskin (1989).

103 *. . . mainstream Jewish tradition* . . . "Mainstream" because Philo already engaged in it in the Talmudic period. But Philo has been embraced far more by Christians than by Jews.

104 *"Rabbi Simeon said"* . . . Zohar III:152a, as quoted in Scholem (1965), p. 64.

104 *. . . drash is the key* . . . I don't mean to diminish the role of *pshat. Pshat* is necessary as a contrast with *drash*, for one thing. It also settles the broad contours of what the text is telling us. *Pshat* gives us our first and guiding sense of what a text means, and thus constrains what counts as a good *drash*.

As we saw above, regarding the stubborn and rebellious son, even a reading that works against the surface level of a text needs to be responsible to the details of that surface level—if we are to take it as a reading of the text at all. One can read the Fool in *King Lear* as a figment of the King's imagination, or as Cordelia in disguise (there are textual clues supporting these readings—the fact that the Fool appears only when the King is mad supports the first of them, and the fact that the Fool appears only when Cordelia is not on stage supports the second). But if one tries to read the Fool as Othello in disguise, one has abandoned the effort to interpret *King Lear* altogether.

109   *. . . coheres with our individual moral and telic intuitions.* A reader for this book has suggested that I arrive here at the position of the Reform rabbi Eugene Borowitz. I had not thought of this when writing the book, nor had I read much Borowitz, but there certainly are affinities: see for instance "The Autonomous Jewish Self," in Borowitz (2002). Here and elsewhere, however, Borowitz gives individual conscience ultimate authority over Jewish law:

> [Jewish law and folkways] do not "command" my sort of liberal Jew, precisely because of their external, heteronomous nature. . . . I and many Jews like me can accept Jewish tradition as guiding us, . . . but not as overriding "conscience." Identifying our dignity as human beings with our autonomy, we are determined to think for ourselves. ("Autonomous Jewish Self," p. 222).,

I see the individual conscience, by contrast, only as a *constraint* on the communal interpretation of Jewish law, which I very much regard as commanding me. Nor is the fact that Jewish law is "external" and "heteronomous" problematic, on my understanding of telic teachings. There is a balance to be struck between authority and autonomy (see p. 113 ff). Borowitz—along with Reform Judaism more generally—lets go too much of the element of authority.

109   *. . . are obligated by our religious commitment itself to leave them . . .* Compare Maimonides (1927), pp. 217–8 (Book of Knowledge, "Hilchot De'ot," 6.1):

> If all the states known to [a man], . . . be followers of a path which is not good, . . . or, if he be unable to migrate to a state whose rules of conduct are good, . . . he should isolate himself and live in seclusion, even as it is said, "Let him sit alone and keep silence." (Lamentations 3:28). And, if the inhabitants of his state be evildoers . . . who deny him the right of residence in the state unless he become assimilated with them, . . . he should go forth and dwell in caves, or cliffs, or deserts . . .

110   *Moses also argues with God . . .* See Exodus 33:14–17, Numbers 11:10–23 and Numbers 14:11–20; Jonah 4; practically all of Job's speeches; and Genesis

32:25–33. It is worth noting that although God calls Job to account for presumption, in the speech out of the whirlwind (Job 38), He also prefers Job's honesty to the blandishments of Job's comforters (Job 42:8). The idea that the God of the Hebrew Bible wants human beings to challenge Him— even to disobey Him—is brought out beautifully in Hazony (2012).

111 *By way of these challenges*... I of course do not mean that the more the text challenges us morally, the better. One can reach a point of feeling that the text is morally untenable—just as one can come to feel that its telic vision is shallow or silly or implausible—and turn away from it, in favor of another religion or none. Many people, understandably I think, do leave the religion of their childhood for reasons of this sort. But *if* one sticks with a religion, if one continues to find its telic vision on the whole decent and compelling, then one can readily view the moral challenges of its foundational text as invitations, from the text's divine or supremely enlightened author, to wrest a different and deeper meaning from it.

112 *James Kugel... puts this point*... Kugel (2008), p. 666

114 *Ludwig Wittgenstein argued*... Wittgenstein (1958), §§ 1–242. There is much debate over how exactly this argument is supposed to work. I follow McDowell (1998).

115 *We all use our judgment*... I explore the importance of judgment in Fleischacker (1999). See especially Chapters 1–4.

115 *... unfolding their true meaning*... For this reason it represents a deep confusion about the nature of revelation when historical scholars insist that a purportedly revealed text be understood in accordance with the intentions of its likely human authors. Marc Brettler, for instance, says that many ritual texts in the Torah "lack an ethical or moral component, and we misunderstand (or 'anachronize') them if we claim that such a component is implicit.": Brettler (2005), p. 83. But insofar as one considers the true author of the text to be God, there is no anachronism in reading it as if it were given to one right now, and no misunderstanding about presuming that what it means may be different for different readers, or change over time.

117 *... restoring something*... See Halivni (1998). For some reservations about Halivni's conclusions, see Fleischacker (2013b).

118 *Chapter 7: Diversity and Respect.* This chapter parallels Fleischacker (2011), Part IV, Chapter 7; the end of the chapter also briefly recapitulates themes explored in Fleischacker (2011), Part V, Chapter 3.

118 ...*religious diversity*... There is a burgeoning contemporary literature on this subject. See, for instance, Hick (1982) and (1985), Griffiths (2001), and Brill (2010) and (2013).

120 ...*must show up in other traditions*... This is the position that today gets called "inclusivism." See Griffiths (2001), for discussion.

120 *More radically, one may believe*... This is the position of JG Herder, the founder of modern cultural pluralism, as regards both religions and cultures. See Fleischacker (1994).

123 ...*the first tablet of the Ten Commandments*... Which is to say, among the five commandments understood by Jews to concern relations between human beings and God, rather than the five concerning relations between one human being and another.

123 ...*taught in a family and a culture.* Inter alia, this makes sense of how we can read the Bible as the word of God even after the discoveries of historical criticism: we can say that even as God made use of human ways of speaking, so He made use of human cultural traditions. In order to "speak in human language," God had to graft His teaching to the Israelites onto the rituals, institutions, and laws they shared with their neighbors. Only a text that worked through the Israelites' cultural surroundings could speak to their emotional and conceptual formation.

This is rather different from the view, once popular among liberal Protestants and Reform Jews, on which the Bible comes increasingly to represent God's will as it comes to be written by increasingly rational Israelites, with the sophisticated civilization by which to transform the crude myths of their past into a properly moral conception of God. On my view, God must speak to people in *any* time and place—including "sophisticated," rationalistic times and places—through images and commands that resonate with the emotional yearnings that history has made salient to those people, not through a purely ahistorical reason. It is not the more rationalistic writings of the prophets and sages, but the insistence on reading all the materials of the Bible as expressing God's will that marks the formation of Judaism, as a powerful religious vision, out of its spiritually and morally shallower past. The Jews transformed their old tales into a vision of God by embracing them as expressions of God's will, and humbling themselves to the attempt to find an appropriately divine meaning for them, not by surveying those materials from above, and pruning them in accordance with a philosophical theory.

The latter approach, advocated by Plato and followed by religious rationalists ever since, makes a shambles of revelation. For such rationalists, nothing can really be revealed; all wisdom must reside within our reason.

An approach that centers on imaginative commitment, on the other hand, can grant that revelation requires a rational reception *of* that revelation while stressing at the same time that we need to receive something from outside ourselves, to see ourselves as not already containing everything that God might want to tell us.

123 *...God's vision for them...* Here and there in the Hebrew Bible, God indicates to the Israelites that he has covenants with other peoples: "'Are you not as the children of the Ethiopians unto Me, O children of Israel?' says the Lord. 'Have not I brought up ... the Philistines from Caphtor, and Aram from Kir?'" (Amos 9:7). Or Deuteronomy 4:19: "And when you lift your eyes to the heaven and see the sun and the moon and the stars..., don't be seduced into bowing down to them or serving them. These the Lord your God apportioned to all the [other] peoples under heaven." See also Malachi 1:11, according to which the sacrifices of all peoples, even if nominally idolatrous, are offered up to God. On attitudes toward other religions in traditional Judaism more generally, see Brill (2010) and (2013).

127 *...implicitly imitating Christ...* The theologian Karl Rahner spoke of such people as "anonymous Christians": see for instance Rahner (1976), p. 283

131 *Finally, people of all religions and none...* The last few pages of this book touch on political themes that I develop in Fleischacker (2011), Part V, Chapter 3. See also Fleischacker (2013), Chapter 11.

131 *Elsewhere I have called this...* In Fleischacker (2013), Chapter 11.

132 *An open public space...* Compare Weithman (2005), pp. 105–6.

133 *...cryptic vision of the good, rooted in a non-naturalistic metaphysics...* In his last book, Ronald Dworkin presented a secular view that more or less meets this description: see Dworkin (2013). He too regarded it as a way of building bridges between secular and religious people.

136 *...breaking off a conversation...* See Genesis 18:1–2 and BT Shabbat 127a.

137 *"Here [is the knight of faith]"...* Kierkegaard (1954), pp. 49–51.

Bibliography

Alston, William. (1993). *Perceiving God*. Ithaca: Cornell University Press.

Aquinas, Thomas. (1953). *The Political Ideas of Thomas Aquinas*. Ed. D Bigongiari. New York: Hafner Press.

Arendt, Hannah. (1968). *Between Past and Future*. Enlarged edition. Harmondsworth: Penguin.

Arendt, Hannah. (1978). *The Life of the Mind*. San Diego: Harcourt Brace Jovanovich.

Aristotle. (1984) *Nicomachean Ethics*. Trans. WD Ross and JO Urmson. In *The Complete Works of Aristotle*. Ed. Jonathan Barnes. Princeton: Princeton University Press.

Beiser, Frederick. (1987). *The Fate of Reason*. Cambridge: Harvard University Press.

Bible. Many editions, including many online versions. I have largely used the JPS Hebrew-English Tanakh, second edition (Philadelphia: Jewish Publication Society, 1999), revising its translations where I felt necessary.

Borowitz, Eugene. (2002). *Studies in the Meaning of Judaism*. Philadelphia: Jewish Publication Society.

Boswell, John. (1980). *Christianity, Social Tolerance and Homosexuality*. Chicago: University of Chicago Press.

Brettler, Marc. (2005). *How to read the Jewish Bible*. Oxford: Oxford University Press.

Brewer, Talbot. (2009). *The Retrieval of Ethics*. Oxford: Oxford University Press.

Brill, Alan. (2010). *Judaism and Other Religions: Models of Understanding*. New York: Palgrave Macmillan.

Brill, Alan. (2013). *Judaism and World Religions: Encountering Christianity, Islam and Eastern Traditions*. New York: Palgrave Macmillan.

BT (Babylonian Talmud). Many editions, including online versions. A generally reliable English translation was published by the Soncino Press in the mid-twentieth century, edited by I Epstein.

Cavell, Stanley. (1979). *The Claim of Reason*. Oxford: Oxford University Press.

Chignell, Andrew. (forthcoming). *What May I Hope? (Kant's Questions)*. London: Routledge.

Donagan, Alan. (1999). *Reflections on Philosophy and Religion*. New York: Oxford University Press.

Dorff, Elliot N. (1996). *Conservative Judaism: Our Ancestors to our Descendants.* Revised edition. New York: United Synagogue of Conservative Judaism.

Dworkin, Ronald. (2013). *Religion Without God.* Cambridge: Harvard University Press.

Easwaran, Eknath. (1987). "Introduction". *The Upanishads.* London: Penguin.

Finley, MI. (1979). *The World of Odysseus.* Harmondsworth: Penguin.

Fleischacker, Samuel. (1994a). "Frustrated Contracts, Poetry and Truth." *Raritan.*

Fleischacker, Samuel. (1994b). *Ethics of Culture.* Ithaca: Cornell University Press.

Fleischacker, Samuel. (1999). *A Third Concept of Liberty: Judgment and Freedom in Kant and Adam Smith.* Princeton: Princeton University Press.

Fleischacker, Samuel. (2011). *Divine Teaching and the Way of the World: A Defense of Revealed Religion.* Oxford: Oxford University Press.

Fleischacker, Samuel. (2013a). *What is Enlightenment? (Kant's Questions).* London: Routledge.

Fleischacker, Samuel. (2013b). "Making Sense of the Revelation at Sinai." The-Torah.com.

Fleischacker, Samuel. (2014). "Two Models for Accepting the Torah." TheTorah. com.

Garfield, Jay. (1995). *The Fundamental Wisdom of the Middle Way.* Trans. and commentator J Garfield. New York: Oxford University Press.

Gaus, Gerald. (2012). *The Order of Public Reason.* Cambridge: Cambridge University Press.

Griffiths, Paul. (2001). *Problems of Religious Diversity.* Oxford: Blackwell.

Habermas, Jürgen. (1995). *Moral Consciousness and Communicative Action.* Trans. C Lenhardt and S Nicholsen. Cambridge: MIT Press.

Haidt, Jonathan. (2006). *The Happiness Hypothesis.* New York: Basic Books.

Halivni, David Weiss. (1998). *Revelation Restored: Divine Writ and Critical Responses.* Boulder: Westview Press.

HaNagid, Shmuel. (1996). *Selected Poems of Shmuel HaNagid.* Trans. and ed. Peter Cole. Princeton: Princeton University Press.

Hazony, Yoram. (2012). *The Philosophy of Hebrew Scripture.* Cambridge: Cambridge University Press.

Heschel, Abraham Joshua. (1955). *God in Search of Man.* New York: Farrar, Straus, and Giroux.

Hick, John. (1982). *God Has Many Names.* Second edition. Philadelphia: Westminster Press.

Hick, John. (1985). *Problems of Religious Pluralism.* New York: Palgrave Macmillan.

Hume, David. (1975). *Enquiry Concerning Human Understanding.* Ed. LA Selby-Bigge and PH Nidditch. Third edition. Oxford: Clarendon Press.

Kant, Immanuel. (1956). *Critique of Practical Reason.* Trans. Lewis White Beck. Indianapolis: Bobbs-Merrill.

Kant, Immanuel. (1998). *Religion Within the Boundaries of Mere Reason.* Trans. and ed. A Wood and G Di Giovanni. Cambridge: Cambridge University Press.

Kierkegaard, Søren. (1954). *Fear and Trembling.* Trans. W Lowrie. Princeton: Princeton University Press.

Kierkegaard, Søren. (1962). *Philosophical Fragments.* Trans. D Swenson and H Hong. Princeton: Princeton University Press.

Kugel, James. (2008). *How to Read the Bible.* New York: Free Press.

Maimonides, Moses. (1927). *Mishneh Torah.* Trans. Simon Glazer. New York: Maimonides Publishing Company.

Maimonides, Moses. (1962). *The Guide of the Perplexed.* Trans. S Pines. Chicago: University of Chicago Press.

McDowell, John. (1998). "Wittgenstein on Following a Rule." In J McDowell, *Mind, Value, and Reality.* Cambridge: Harvard University Press.

Mendelssohn, Moses. (1983). *Jerusalem.* Hanover: University Press of New England.

Meta, Gita. (1993). *A River Sutra.* New York: Vintage.

Nachmanides, Moses. (1974). *Commentary on the Torah.* Trans. Rabbi Charles Chavel. New York: Shilo Publishing House.

Oppenheimer, Mark. "Examining the Growth of the 'Spiritual but Not Religious.'" *New York Times.* July 17, 2014.

Plantinga, Alvin. (1993). *Warrant and Proper Function.* Oxford: Oxford University Press.

Plantinga, Alvin.(2000). *Warranted Christian Belief.* Oxford: Oxford University Press.

Plantinga, Alvin.(2011). *Where the Conflict Really Lies: Science, Religion and Naturalism.* Oxford: Oxford University Press.

Plato. (1997). *Complete Works.* Ed. J Cooper. Indianapolis: Hackett Publishing Company.

Rahner, Karl. (1976). *Theological Investigations.* Vol. 14. Trans. D Bourke. London: Darton, Longman, & Todd.

Rahula, Walpola. (1974). *What the Buddha Taught.* Second edition. New York: Grove Press.

Riskin, Shlomo. (1989). *Women and Jewish Divorce.* Hoboken: Ktav Publishing.

Scanlon, TM. (1998). *What We Owe To Each Other.* Cambridge: Harvard University Press.

Scholem, Gershom. (1965). *On the Kabbalah and Its Symbolism.* New York: Schocken.

Singer, Peter. (1995). *How Are We to Live?* Amherst, NY: Prometheus Books.

Stevens, Wallace. (2011). "Anecdote of the Jar." In *The Collected Poems of Wallace Stevens*. New York: Random House.

Swinburne, Richard. (1992). *Revelation: From Metaphor to Analogy*. Oxford: Clarendon Press.

Swinburne, Richard. (2004). *The Existence of God*. Oxford: Oxford University Press.

Taylor, Charles. (1984). "Rationality." In *Rationality and Relativism*. Ed. M Hollis and S Lukes. Cambridge: The MIT Press.

Tolstoy, Leo. (1981). *The Death of Ivan Ilyich*. Trans. L Solotaroff. New York: Bantam.

Tolstoy, Leo. (1983). *Confession*. Trans. D Patterson. New York: WW Norton.

Weithman, Paul. (2005). "Why Should Christians Endorse Human Rights?" In T Cuneo (ed.), *Religion in the Liberal Polity*. Notre Dame: University of Notre Dame Press.

Williams, Bernard. (1985). *Ethics and the Limits of Philosophy*. Cambridge: Harvard University Press.

Wittgenstein, Ludwig. (1958). *Philosophical Investigations*. Trans. GEM Anscombe. New York: Macmillan.

Wittgenstein, Ludwig. (1977). *On Certainty*. Ed. GEM Anscombe and GH von Wright. Trans. Denis Paul and GEM Anscombe. Oxford: Basil Blackwell.

Index